prof. Slomansen - another p...
Cal Western (→ SD) . whett...
now...

Boyle: ICJ statute .

publicists - good secondary authority.

jug. Constitut...
former member
Polish Sup.
Ct .
S U.

In re:

MORE THAN 50,000 NUCLEAR WEAPONS

LEXIS/NEXIS.

(1) oral argument - any witness?)

(2) write ups - impact

2 articles in LATimes)
1 before a couple yrs.
reporter to trial. Ind. - down near airport.
appeal after P's - 2 others -

LA Daily Journal
front pg. article.
amicus.
statements from professor

all day trial videotaped.

video - small booklet. Nuclear A

4 all based on. asked court to take judicial
notice of nature of nuke weapons

jurisdiction in I.H, merits of legal issues -

In re:

More Than 50,000 Nuclear Weapons

Analyses of the Illegality of Nuclear Weapons Under International Law

Francis A. Boyle, Alfred P. Rubin, Burns H. Weston
Sean MacBride, Richard A. Falk, Dorothy Hodgkin
Maurice Wilkins, Peter Weiss

With an introduction by Burns H. Weston

ALETHEIA PRESS

1991

Aletheia Press
P.O. Box 1178
Northampton, Massachusetts 01061

Manufactured in the United States of America

Library of Congress Cataloging-in-Publication Data

Boyle, Francis Anthony, 1950-
    In re: More than 50,000 nuclear weapons : analyses of the
illegality of nuclear weapons under international law / Francis A.
Boyle, Alfred P. Rubin, Burns H. Weston : with an introduction by
Burns H. Weston.
        p.   cm.
    ISBN 0–9623718–4–X (lib. bdg.) : $30.00.—ISBN 0–9623718–5–8
(pbk.) : $12.00
    1. Nuclear weapons (International law)   I. Rubin, Alfred P.
 II. Weston, Burns H., 1933-   . III. Title.   IV. Title: More than
50,000 nuclear weapons.
JX5133.A7B69 1991
341.7'34—dc20   91–2294
                                                            CIP

Contents

Contributors

Francis A. Boyle is a Professor of Law and Member of the Program in Arms Control, Disarmament and International Security at the University of Illinois in Champaign.

Alfred P. Rubin is a Professor of International Law, Fletcher School of Law and Diplomacy at Tufts University.

Burns H. Weston is Bessie Dutton Murray Professor of Law at The University of Iowa College of Law.

Sean MacBride (1904–88) Chair of the London Nuclear Warfare Tribunal, was a co-founder of Amnesty International, Chair of AI's International Executive (1961–75), Assistant Secretary General of the United Nations (1973–77), and Nobel Peace Prize recipient (1974).

Richard A. Falk, Member of the London Nuclear Warfare Tribunal, is Albert G. Milbank Professor of International Law and Practice at Princeton University.

Dorothy Hodgkin, Member of the London Nuclear Warfare Tribunal, is Professor Emeritus and Fellow of Wolfson College at Oxford, and a Nobel Prize recipient for Chemistry (1964).

Maurice Wilkins, Member of the London Nuclear Warfare Tribunal, is Professor Emeritus of Biophysics and Fellow of Kings College, and a Nobel Prize recipient for Medicine (1962).

Peter Weiss is the Founder and Chair of the Lawyers Committee on Nuclear Policy (New York) and co-founder of the International Association of Lawyers Against Nuclear Arms (IALANA).

Foreword

We know that nuclear weapons are immoral, their purpose being to threaten the death of hundreds of millions of innocent people. We can also deduce that nuclear weapons are undemocratic because they focus power in the hands of a small number of persons. Many argue that these weapons undermine the U.S. Constitution by effectively removing the war-making power from the Congress. Military leaders, including Douglas MacArthur, have concluded that nuclear weapons are also suicidal. Philosophers have gone further and reasoned that these weapons are "omnicidal," having the power to destroy all.

To these arguments in opposition to developing and maintaining nuclear arsenals, legal scholars add the proposition that nuclear weapons are illegal under international law. The judicial opinions expressed in this collection are not easily enforceable, but they tell us clearly that international law prohibits the use or threatened use of weapons of indiscriminate mass destruction. Thus, these legal conclusions will only have effect to the extent that they influence public opinion—the court of last resort.

I urge the reader to study these opinions and judge for yourself the legality of nuclear weapons. As citizens of a nuclear armed nation, each of us bears the responsibility to take necessary actions to bring government military policies into line with international law.

David Krieger
President, Nuclear Age Peace Foundation
Santa Barbara, California

Preface to the Boyle-Rubin-Weston Opinions

Let us assume that we have learned of a planet, Alpha, in a distant galaxy, where intelligent life abounds. We have also learned that Alpha is divided into two major military powers, each of which possesses weapons so powerful that, if used, would destroy all life for thousands of years. Further, we have learned that the power to use the terrible weapons ultimately resides in the hands of one person in each military domain. Finally, we have learned that the highly developed legal system on Alpha has never rendered an opinion as to the legality or illegality of the weapons, since the courts defer, in matters of military decision-making, to the military leaders themselves.

What could be said about such a planet: The living beings on Alpha are crazy; such a situation is understandable and justifiable; or the legal system on Alpha needs to be developed further, so the issues concerning these weapons can be judicially reviewed.

Obviously, just such considerations trouble many persons on our planet, but our situation is not as easy to discuss as Alpha's since we have become numbed to the presence of nuclear weapons. Indeed, a majority of the humans on Earth were born after the Hiroshima detonation, and know only the world of nuclear standoff.

Much has been written about the horrors of nuclear war. An estimated 2.2 billion persons could be killed outright by a major nuclear war, according to the World Health Organization. Can any attorney truly argue that this is not a case for an injunction against such an unbelievable horror?

Surprisingly, until I undertook to bring such a case before a judicial tribunal, not a single lawsuit squarely addressed the issues of the legality or illegality of the threat of use or actual use of nuclear weapons, and the research, development, production, stockpiling, transporting and support functions related to such weapons.

The Provisional District World Court

It became clear, after some research, that bringing a lawsuit in a state or federal court in the United States would not result in a ruling on the merits, since domestic courts consider such issues as the legality of nuclear weapons to be "political questions" which require abstention. Turning to the International Court of Justice in the Hague, under the United Nations Charter, likewise seemed futile, since defendants in any suit must agree to the jurisdiction of the Court, and only nations can sue.

How then to do it? It was necessary to search for a court that was empowered to hear such matters. And it came to pass that such a court was in a formative stage, within a provisional world government, called the Federation of Earth. Under its Constitution, a complete court system could be formed. Upon my urging, a Bill was passed at the Federation's First Provisional World Parliament in Brighton, England, in 1982, establishing such a court in Los Angeles. The lawsuit was filed soon thereafter, on behalf of all of the persons of Earth, against twenty-eight "nuclear" nations. The defendants were divided into three groups: the superpowers, the nuclear host nations, and the nuclear-capable nations.

Every step of the process was conducted with meticulous care to conform to generally accepted legal procedures. The defendant nations were served numerous times with legal pleadings. (India was the only state to file a responsive pleading, stating that it was against the use of nuclear weapons.) Attorney Gaither Kodis of Bellevue, Washington, was appointed to serve as an *amicus* to the Court, representing the viewpoint of the defendants in briefs and oral argument.

Prestigious Three-Judge Panel Appointed

During the almost six-year duration of the lawsuit, perhaps the most dramatic event, other than the court hearing itself, was the appointment of three highly qualified judges to the panel who were to decide the case: Judge Francis A. Boyle, Professor of Law at the University of Illinois Law School at Champaign; Judge Alfred P. Rubin, Professor of International Law at the School of Law and Diplomacy at Tufts University; and Judge Burns H. Weston, Bessie Dutton Murray Professor of Law at The University of Iowa School of Law. The fact that the three judges are leading experts in the field of nuclear-weapons law resulted in the three lengthy opinions having a far-reaching legal effect. As Judge Boyle stated in his opinion:

> Under article 38(1)(d) of the Statute of the International Court of Justice, this Opinion constitutes a "subsidiary means for the determination of rules of law." It could therefore be relied upon by some future international war crimes tribunal.

The article 38(1)(d) impact of the three opinions cannot be overemphasized, since, as the only legal proceeding on the subject, *In re: More than 50,000 Nuclear Weapons* stands as the seminal case in the field.

Injunction Granted

The essence of the area of major agreement among the three judges was that each found that the rules of war do indeed govern nuclear weapons, and these rules prohibit their use or threat of use under virtually all conditions presently contemplated by the superpowers. To support these holdings, all three judges granted the injunction requested by plaintiffs, prohibiting such use and threat of use of nuclear weapons. Two of the three judges also stated that planning for a nuclear war was prohibited.

Initial reactions from the international legal community were quite favorable. It now remains to be seen how the opinions influence military policy of the defendant nuclear nations.

The Far-Reaching Effect of the Illegality of Nuclear Weapons

It will only take a few persons to start a peaceful international protest against nuclear weapons that can ultimately impact on the very core of nuclear policy. Remember the pioneering work of Linus Pauling against atmospheric testing and the crusade of Helen Caldicott against nuclear arsenals. Those who follow can now cite to the authority of the Boyle-Rubin-Weston opinions. Each person reading these opinions can pass the message of the illegality to others, and one day those who can press the buttons will refuse to do so, if, for no other reason, out of fear of being tried as war criminals. We are a people of law, a planet of law. We now have the law on the most horrible of weapons. Let us observe it.

Leon Vickman, Esq.
Encino, California

Introduction

International Law and World Peace: The Professional Challenge

Burns H. Weston

To a joint session of Congress early in the 1990–91 Persian Gulf crisis, President George Bush declared: "Today [a] new world is struggling to be born. A world quite apart from the one we have known. A world where the rule of law supplants the rule of the jungle…America and the world must support the rule of law."[1] Throughout the crisis, both to condemn Iraq and to rally worldwide resistance against Iraq's crimes, the President returned to this invocation of international law. Indeed, not content to rely simply on the use of force prohibitions of the U.N. Charter, he and his administration even cited the post-World War II Nuremberg principles prohibiting crimes against the peace, war crimes, and crimes against humanity. With the exception of Mikhail Gorbachev's December 1988 address to the United Nations, one has to search for statements earlier in this century—by Woodrow Wilson, Henry L. Stimson, Maxim Litvinov, Winston Churchill, and Franklin Delano Roosevelt—to find anything comparable.

Regrettably, however, it is possible to be cynical about this sort of talk. No matter how tempting the President's call for a "new world order" based on respect for international law and a cooperating United Nations might be, particularly in the face of Iraq's treachery, the history of U.S. foreign policy, especially in recent decades, warrants major skepticism.[2] Nevertheless, peace activists should take heart; they should seize upon this presidential endorsement and press their case to the utmost. It is these very same Nuremberg Principles and related norms of restraint upon the use of force in international relations that challenge the legality of nuclear weapons and the nuclear deterrence strategies that provide for their manufacture and deployment. It is these very same principles and norms that, ever since the beginning of the Atomic Age, have helped to energize our sense of moral—and prudent—statecraft.

In 1955, for example, on the tenth anniversary of the dropping of the first nuclear bomb on Hiroshima, the English philosopher Bertrand Russell, with the prior counsel and endorsement of Albert Einstein, issued a declaration that, it was hoped, would stimulate nations and governments to renounce nuclear weapons and the spiralling arms race, in keeping with the principles and norms that were established in San Francisco and at Nuremberg a decade earlier. This Russell-Einstein manifesto, as it came to be called, read in part as follows:[3]

> We are speaking on this occasion, not as members of this or that nation, continent or creed, but as human beings, members of the species of man,[4] whose continued existence is in doubt…[W]e want you, if you can, to…consider yourselves only as members of a biological species which has had a remarkable history, and whose disappearance none of us can desire.
>
> We have to learn to think in a new way. We have to learn to ask ourselves, not what steps can be taken to give military victory to whatever group we prefer, for there no longer are such steps; the question we have to ask ourselves is: What steps can be taken to prevent a military contest of which the issue must be disastrous to all parties?
>
> Many warnings have been uttered by eminent men of science and by authorities in military strategy. None of them will say that the worst results are certain. What they do say is that these results are possible, and no one can be sure that they will not be realized. We have not yet found that the views of experts depend in any degree upon their politics or prejudices. They depend only, so far as our researches have revealed, upon the extent of the particular expert's knowledge. We have found that the men who know most are the most gloomy.
>
> There lies before us, if we choose, continual progress in happiness, knowledge and wisdom. Shall we, instead, choose death, because

we cannot forget our quarrels? We appeal, as human beings, to human beings: Remember your humanity and forget the rest. If you can do so, the way lies open to a new paradise; if you cannot, there lies before you the risk of universal death.

Nine world-renowned scientists publicly endorsed this declaration in addition to Russell and Einstein. All but two of the total of eleven were Nobel Prize recipients.

Tragically, the world community—particularly its governing elites—did not take these words seriously to heart. Indeed, despite the aggravated mutilations we call Hiroshima-Nagasaki and despite subsequent appeals to sanity, it greeted them with a deafening silence, either refusing to face squarely the catastrophic dangers inherent in nuclear weaponry or relegating these dangers to the periphery of responsible attention whenever the possibility of nuclear confrontation seemed real. For decades humanity lived in the shadow of the valley of death and said little about it.

Then came, however, President Ronald Reagan in the early-1980s, threatening military confrontation with the "Evil Empire," sending psychological shockwaves around the world. Soon thereafter, with the International Physicians for the Prevention of Nuclear War, the National [U.S.] Conference of Catholic Bishops, and others first helping to sound and clarify the alarm,[5] the complex questions surrounding nuclear weapons and warfare began to emerge from the inner chambers of the physicists and strategists to become visible and urgent to the common man and woman. And with the creation of the Lawyers Alliance for Nuclear Arms Control[6] and the Lawyers Committee on Nuclear Policy in the United States,[7] and equivalent associations elsewhere, they began to become visible and urgent to legal professionals as well.

The chapters in this volume constitute some of the important formal responses that have issued from the legal profession regarding nuclear weapons and warfare in recent years. They highlight the still too little known fact that an already substantial but still growing body of international legal opinion is persuaded that the use and threat of use of nuclear weapons are in virtually all instances incompatible with the core precepts of international law.[8] Chapter 1 presents the deliberative results of a 1988 challenge to the legality of nuclear weapons before a "Provisional District World Court" organized under the Constitution of the Federation of Earth.[9] Chapter 2 contains excerpts from the 1988 joint opinion of the *ad hoc* London Nuclear Warfare Tribunal.[10] Chapter 3 sets forth the 1990 *Statement on the Illegality of Nuclear Warfare* of the New York-based Lawyers Committee on Nuclear Policy.[11] And chapter 4 restates the 1989 Hague Declaration on the illegality of nuclear weapons of the Stockholm-based International Association of Lawyers Against Nuclear Arms (IALANA).[12]

The exact utility of these thoughtful and persuasive testimonials as sources of international law, I concede, may be open to some debate, as they are the product of unofficial arrangements and procedures. Nevertheless, they clearly constitute "subsidiary means for the determination of rules of law" within the meaning of Article 38 of the Statute of the International Court of Justice,[13] capable of being relied upon by some future international war crimes tribunal. Also, even when it is not possible to appeal successfully to the formal structures of government, they help to mobilize political energies and movements that seek to expose the illegality—even the criminality—of official nuclearist policy. Separately and together, they take seriously President Bush's call for a "new world order" based on respect for international law.

And none too soon! The revolutionary changes that rocked Eastern Europe and the Soviet Union—indeed, the world!—beginning in 1989-90, and that continue to do so as we hurtle to the end of the twentieth century, have rendered obsolete the political and military arrangements that assisted European and wider world security for over four decades following World War II. The Soviet Union, home to more than 25,000 nuclear weapons and many newly-awakened nationalisms, faces a world history that demonstrates little support for the proposition that collapsing empires fade quietly. And in our increasingly high-tech world, with military research and development (R&D) fast at work on atomic guns, particle-beam cannons, and other space-age deviltries that divert attention from the perils of nuclear proliferation, dozens of regimes in Western Asia and elsewhere have been acquiring nuclear and other weapons of mass destruction—and the means to deliver them to almost anywhere on earth—with frightening ease and speed. Not to be overlooked either is the unabated intensity with which the United States and to a lesser extent the Soviet Union pursue the modernization of their strategic arsenals and the ease with which, during the Persian Gulf war, commentators were able to recommend the use of nuclear weapons, eroding the taboo against them.[14]

In sum, the need for a nuclear weapons-free world and a global regime to support it is mandatory in the most pressing sense, and the more compelling because of these and related developments. With the possible exception of ozone depletion, global warming, and related environmental concerns, nothing is more menacing to the well-being of our planet than the sincerely communicated threat to use nuclear weapons if and when sufficiently provoked.

It is essential to understand, however, that a nuclear weapons-free world requires far more than the kinds of "deep cuts" and related arms reductions proposals that were recommended in the 1978 Final Act of the First U.N. General Assembly Special Session on Disarmament,[15] and in the so-called Five Continent Initiative's Delhi Declaration issued by the Heads of State of Argentina, Greece, India, Mexico, Sweden, and Tanzania in January 1985[16] (proposals that have been the subject of some hopeful but still outrageously hesitant discussions between the Soviet Union and the United States in recent years). Even heightened adherence to the already existing norms of restraint upon the transnational use of force that are cited in the quasi-judicial and quasi-parliamentary judgments that make up this volume falls short of the full measure of legal and policy criteria that is required to help bring an essentially nuclear weapons-free world into being. Necessary as these and like initiatives are, what is needed, and what peace activists must now demand, is an entire complex of policy initiatives—legal, political, economic, military, and otherwise—that jointly can protect against international violence in such a way as will make it unnecessary for States to rely on nuclear and other weapons of mass destruction to safeguard their security.

Elsewhere I have helped identify some of the mix of "alternative security" policy initiatives that can work to this end.[17] Here I review some of the legal policy initiatives—normative, procedural, and institutional—that may be counted among them.[18] I do so because, having established more or less the illegality and criminality of nuclear weapons and warfare, it is now time for lawyers—and peace activists in general—to move the antinuclear struggle forward to a new level of concern, toward achieving a broad consensus on the design and construction of a global security system that can ensure the sanctity and stability of life without dependency on the nuclear threat. Conflict is likely to be violently expressed in the world system for years to come, and as a consequence people are not going to be easily dissuaded from a nuclear deterrence system that seems to have protected them for better than four decades. Therefore, there must be established an effective alternative or set of alternatives to nuclear deterrence as a means of dealing with national and international security. Otherwise, there will be no getting rid of the nuclear habit. Otherwise, there will be no real progress toward genuine and lasting peace.

Normative Policy Initiatives

Four normative regimes come immediately to mind as capable of assisting a nuclear weapons-free international system for which peace activists, lawyer and non-lawyer alike, should strive.

1.   A Comprehensive Nuclear Weapons Ban[19]

The enforcement of existing legal norms that interdict virtually all currently planned uses of nuclear weapons is seriously encumbered by a tradition of political leadership—Machiavellian in character—that typically indulges self-serving interpretations of the legal status of controversial uses of force. A pervasive subjectivity in world politics makes it exceedingly hazardous to tie restraint *vis-a-vis* nuclear weapons to characterizations of warfare as "defensive" or "aggressive," these labels commonly masking politically congenial and politically hostile uses of force. Thus, a comprehensive anti-nuclear weapons regime is needed.

Such a regime would embrace at least the following:

a.   an absolute prohibition on first strike and other destabilizing weapons and weapons systems—land-based, sea-based, and air-launched—because such weapons and weapons systems increase the pressure to launch on warning and thereby increase the possibility of nuclear war by accident or miscalculation;

b. a declaration that all R&D, war plans, strategic doctrines, and strategic threats having first-strike characteristics are illegal *per se*, and that all persons knowingly associated with them are deemed engaged in a continuing criminal enterprise;

c. a presumption that virtually any actual use of nuclear weapons, particularly a first use of such weapons (even in a defensive mode), but also a second or retaliatory "countervalue" use (against cities and other civilian targets), violates the international law of war and constitutes a "crime against humanity";

d. an unequivocal obligation on the part of all States to pursue nuclear disarmament and otherwise minimize the role of nuclear weapons in inter-State conflict (per Article VI of the Treaty on the Non-Proliferation of Nuclear Weapons)[20] by way of, *inter alia*, (i) a renunciation of the policy of first use and the war-fighting doctrines and capabilities that accompany it, (ii) a comprehensive nuclear test ban (CTB), and (iii) strengthened nuclear non-proliferation regimes;

e. a commitment to a strengthened Anti-Ballistic Missile Treaty[21] (because pursuit of an anti-ballistic missile defense system stimulates competition in offensive weapons) together with a ban on all space weapons and space-based missile defense systems (because such systems, especially if not preceded by deep cuts in offensive ballistic missiles, are likely to encourage a proliferation of the most destabilizing weapons and weapons systems); and

f. a clear mandate for all citizens to take whatever steps may be available to them, including acts of nonviolent civil resistance, to expose the illegality of the use of nuclear weapons and to otherwise insist upon the lawful conduct of the foreign policies of their own governments.

A comprehensive nuclear weapons ban such as this, it should be understood, would cause even the "minimum deterrence" strategies currently popular to be legally, if not also morally, suspect.

2.   A Comprehensive Ban on Non-Nuclear Weapons of Mass Destruction

The same arguments that warrant a comprehensive ban on nuclear weapons compel also a comprehensive ban on non-nuclear weapons of mass destruction, *chemical and biological weapons included.* In addition, a ban on such weapons would lessen the prospect that a belligerent State, especially a beleaguered one, might establish or renew a dependence upon nuclear weapons. Mirroring the "Comprehensive Nuclear Weapons Ban" outlined above, it would include at least the following:

a.   an absolute prohibition on the development, production, stockpiling, and use of conventional mass destruction weapons and weapons systems, including chemical and biological weapons of mass destruction; (i) a strengthened Geneva Gas Protocol,[22] prohibiting the possession as well as the use of the gas and bacteriological methods of warfare covered by the Protocol, and (ii) a strengthened Biological Weapons Convention,[23] providing for effective on-site inspections and enforcement mechanisms capable of responding to scientific advances and new biological technologies;

b.   a declaration that all R&D, war plans, strategic doctrines, and strategic threats having non-nuclear mass destructive characteristics are illegal *per se*, and that all persons knowingly associated with them are deemed engaged in a continuing criminal enterprise;

c.   a presumption that virtually any actual use of such weapons (even in a defensive mode), but also a second or retaliatory use (against cities and other civilian targets), violates the international law of war and constitutes a "crime against humanity";

d.   an unequivocal obligation on the part of all States to eliminate all non-nuclear weapons of mass destruction from their arsenals, including chemical and biological weapons of mass destruction, and otherwise to minimize the role of such weapons in inter-State conflict; and

e.   a clear mandate for all citizens to take whatever steps may be available to them, including acts of nonviolent civil resistance, to expose the illegality of the use of non-nuclear weapons of mass destruction and otherwise to insist upon the lawful conduct of the foreign policies of their own governments.

The point of these limitations, it should be understood, is to restrict all military strategy to a non-offensive/non-provocative defense posture exclusively. Only such an arrangement will permit States to resist the temptation to resort to nuclear weapons.

3.   A Conventional Weapons Non-Proliferation Regime

Just as there has been a proliferation of nuclear weapons since 1945, so has there been a proliferation in the manufacture and export of conventional weapons, particularly to the Third World. This fact is well known. Yet, notwithstanding that this traffic in conventional arms increases not only the destructiveness of conflict but also the likelihood of bloody conflict erupting, the world community stands by and does essentially nothing.

The world community is negligent, however, at great peril to itself. Just as conventional arms are "trip wires" to conventional wars, so are conventional wars—and their arms—"trip wires" to nuclear conflict, capable of engaging nuclear powers and thereby risking escalation to nuclear war. In the absence of a ban on the manufacture and export of conventional weapons, a nuclear weapons-free world would be similarly endangered. To the extent that, in such a world, conventional wars could seriously jeopardize the real and perceived interests of nuclear-prone States, so too could they serve as catalysts to the "reinvention" and subsequent actual use of nuclear weapons to safeguard those interests.

Thus, a conventional weapons non-proliferation regime, greatly limiting if not altogether prohibiting conventional arms traffic, would seem as much a necessity to a post-nuclear global security system as the existing non-proliferation regime is to the present day nuclear deterrence system. It seems particularly a necessity relative to such large and potentially provocative weapons and weapons systems as tanks, armored cars, warships, long-range "attack" aircraft, missiles, and other components of "forward defense." In addition to being the most easily regulated because they are the most easily detected, these large weapons and weapons systems are, among conventional weapons systems, the most capable of contributing to mass destruction. At the very least, such a regime should ensure an effective surveillance and record-keeping system, capable minimally of alerting responsible elites to the presence of dangerous world practices and trends.

4.   A Nuclear Superpower Nonintervention Regime

It is clear that the current nuclear deterrence system operating between the two nuclear superpowers is in reality a system of extended deterrence, meant to guard against far more than intercontinental strategic attacks. Despite the Cold War thaw, both the reconstituted Soviet Union and the United States maintain strong interests in preserving their respective spheres of influence (however defined beyond uncertain borders). But it is clear, too, that this extended deterrence system is of necessity nuclear because, as is now being made increasingly manifest, the economies of neither the United States nor the reconstituted Soviet Union can afford, without major domestic sacrifice, a conventional one. Thus, because the strong economic and political interests of the two powers will not easily go away—and, indeed, may become even more "vital" to them as they ever more discover that they are unable to control people and events as they once did—a post-nuclear global security system must include as one of its cornerstones a nuclear superpower compact to refrain from sending any of their armed forces into the other's clear sphere of influence or into any nonaligned country, even if invited. At the risk of implying approval of superpower spheres of influence, a mutual promise of self-restraint on the part of both the nuclear superpowers, especially one that would ensure their observance of the territorial integrity and political independence of Third World countries, would go a long way toward guaranteeing the viability of a post-nuclear global security system. For those occasions when force may be needed to prevent or minimize deprivations of fundamental human rights and freedoms, recourse to the global and regional intergovernmental organizations that are designed to police such matters should be pursued, in accordance with right process and on a genuinely multilateral basis.[24]

Procedural Policy Initiatives

A global security system that forswears reliance upon nuclear weapons can provide no security at all without clearly established and respected procedures for both peacekeeping and peacemaking. If inter-State disputes can be prevented from degenerating into armed hostilities or settled by peaceful means, they are unlikely to escalate into threats to the peace or acts of aggression and war. It is true that the past record of undertakings to keep the peace under the aegis of the United Nations and to achieve dispute settlement through international tribunals, arbitration, and similar peaceful means has not been very encouraging, not even during the 1990-91 Persian Gulf crisis.[25] But established and respected procedures for multilateral peacekeeping and for the mediation, conciliation, arbitration, and adjudication of international disputes, preferably within the framework of the United Nations but desirable also at the regional level, would seem nevertheless necessary even if not sufficient for the maintenance of world peace and security. Without the active participation of States in peaceful efforts to accommodate each other, there is little likelihood of achieving the stability and harmony that a world free of nuclear weapons would require.

Thus, the following modest procedural initiatives would seem necessary and useful (perhaps especially at the early stages of international accommodation and nuclear disarmament). Again, peace activists, lawyer and non-lawyer, should work toward their realization.

1.   Improvement of U.N. Peacekeeping Opportunities and Capabilities

United Nations peacekeeping opportunities and capabilities can be improved by:[26]

a.   *facilitating automatic peacekeeping action* on the basis of predetermined levels of crisis or thresholds of conflict, thus avoiding the obstructions posed by the exercise of the Security Council veto;

b.   *assuring peacekeeping finances* on an automatic basis, thus again avoiding the obstructions posed by the exercise of the Security Council veto;

c. *guaranteeing military units* (land, sea, and air) on a more or less permanent standby basis (as envisaged in U.N. Charter Article 43), trained for peacekeeping by the member States in the course of their militaries' basic training and on the basis of expertise and additional training provided by an appropriate U.N. agency;

d. *regularly stockpiling military equipment and supplies* needed to enhance the U.N.'s capacity to undertake peacekeeping operations on short notice;

e. *ensuring access to conflict areas* without requiring the initial or continuing permission of the conflicting parties; and

f. *tying U.N. peacekeeping to peacemaking* (i.e. pacific settlement) to ensure that the merits of any given dispute will receive the attention that is needed to achieve long-term stability in the troubled area.

2. Improvement of U.N. and Other Peacemaking Opportunities and Capabilities

United Nations peacemaking opportunities and capabilities can be improved by:[27]

a. *enhancing and making greater use of U.N. dispute settlement mechanisms*, most of which have been rarely if ever used;

b. *encouraging increased consent to mediation, conciliation, arbitration, and adjudication* via (i) guarantees limiting the scope of the third-party judgment to the determination of the doctrines, principles, and rules that could guide the parties in approaching settlement; and (ii) greater use of technically non-binding advisory opinions;

c. *increasing reliance on private persons and nongovernmental organizations* (NGOs) as neutral intermediaries (thereby helping to avoid escalating arguments to full-scale inter-State disputes) in pre-dispute consultations, in post-dispute negotiated settlements, and before international tribunals for the purpose of clarifying a customary law norm or a clause in an international agreement;

d. *convening periodic regional conferences on security and cooperation* similar to the one launched in Helsinki for Europe in 1975 to reflect the priorities and circumstances of the separate regions and, with help from the U.N. Secretariat, to serve the essential decision function of appraisal and recommendation not only on matters relating directly to international security but on economic, social, and cultural matters upon which international security commonly depends; and

e. *adopting a code of international peacemaking procedures* (drawn from a variety of existing instruments) that would allow governmental officials to develop confidence in available procedures and that States could accept as binding upon them in whole or in part.

3.   Improvement of Opportunities and Capabilities for Legal Challenges to Coercive Foreign Policies

Opportunities and capabilities for legal challenges to coercive foreign policies can be improved by:

a. *enhancing the role of the International Court of Justice* relative to threats to the peace, breaches of the peace, and acts of aggression through, for example, (i) expanded acceptance of the Court's compulsory jurisdiction and greater use of its advisory jurisdiction relative to actual or potential hostilities between States; (ii) broadened standing to petition the Court to permit access by qualified nongovernmental organizations; and (iii) increased appeal to the Court's specialized "chamber procedure" in respect of inter-State conflicts unresolved by more local remedies;

b. *facilitating application of the international law of peace in domestic courts* through, for example, the reduction of barriers to "legal standing" on the part of private litigants especially and the narrowing of doctrines of non-justiciability (e.g., the "political question," "act of State," and "sovereign immunity" doctrines) to encourage public accountability in the conduct of foreign policy.

Of course, all of these and similar procedural initiatives have their share of difficulties: winning the confidence of contentious sovereign powers; achieving genuine neutrality in disputes; maintaining effective communication; overcoming legal and political isolationism; and so forth. Nevertheless, all are worthwhile initiatives to pursue because they enhance the prospects for international peace and security.

Institutional Policy Initiatives

At least six institutional initiatives recommend themselves to the farsighted peace activist, some operating perhaps within the framework of the United Nations, some perhaps outside that framework.[28] They of course do not exhaust the institutional policy options that might be recommended. Nonetheless, those that follow seem especially worthy of responsible peace activist attention.

1. *Establish an international disarmament verification agency* which, through satellite observation, seismic and atmospheric surveillance, and on-site inspection, could supplement national means of verification and be capable of transnational monitoring of world military capabilities and movements.[29] Such an agency, with a membership comprising non-nuclear as well as nuclear weapons States, would (a) oversee the implementation of arms control and arms reduction agreements; (b) provide an impartial means of detecting and guarding against the secret testing and production of nuclear weapons and other weapons of mass destruction, including chemical and biological weapons; (c) discourage provocative military buildups and maneuvers; and (d) otherwise acquire the vital experience and reliability needed if arms reductions are ever to proceed very far. As a means of achieving genuine effectiveness, it also would be expected to establish regional oversight boards with authority to conduct on-site inspections of any and all weapons-capable facilities at the request of any State party or qualified nongovernmental organization.

2. *Create an international technological development and weapons program agency* to (a) foster joint research of defensive technologies by multilateral teams of scientists and (b) prevent and restrain arms buildups. Such an organ would provide the

reconstituted Soviet Union and the United States with the opportunity to share defensive technology and to facilitate missile defense research without imperiling the ABM Treaty[30] or otherwise exacerbating the arms race. Also, it could reduce inclinations to surprise the other side with new and threatening developments. As such it could help solidify the new turning point in world affairs that came about with the advent of *glasnost* and *perestroika.*

3.   *Create risk-reduction opportunities and capabilities* by establishing, for example, (a) a joint inter-State consultation commission with a permanent staff composed of the nationals of disputing parties (among others) capable of handling actual and potential conflicts by way of routine review rather than the usual procedure of consulting only in extraordinary circumstances; (b) a joint inter-State negotiating commission composed of nationals from each side of a conflict, working together to find a solution acceptable to all concerned; (c) regional mediation, conciliation, and arbitration panels composed of persons of recognized competence and fair mindedness with authority to investigate and seek the resolution of conflicts and disputes otherwise capable of culminating in hostilities. Where these "local remedies" do not succeed, then appeal should be had to the International Court of Justice for final and binding resolution of the disputes in question. In any event, the common primary purpose of these risk-reduction remedies would be to facilitate communication between contending parties to avert the possibility of war through miscalculation or misperception.

4.   *Create an international "weapons into plowshares" agency* through which the conversion of national arms industries to socially redemptive production could be facilitated and a concrete connection between those who spend resources on armaments and those in economic and technological need could be fruitfully established. The overriding purpose of such an agency, which among other things could help bring labor unions and industrial management together in common enterprise, would be to encourage a comprehensive process of reconstruction and renewal conducive to the establishment of a genuinely productive and equitable world economy that, in turn, would greatly reduce the likelihood that nations would do military battle with one another.

5.   *Create permanent global or regional police forces* consisting of persons recruited individually instead of from national military contingents (as in past U.N. peacekeeping experience), each with loyalty to world or regional authorities rather than national authorities. Such forces would be unencumbered by divided loyalties and by the possibility of sudden, unanticipated recall or withdrawal by national governments (as has happened with *ad hoc* U.N. forces in the Middle East, for example). As a consequence, they would be more readily available, more subject to efficient coordination, and thus more effective overall. As such, better positioned to establish useful precedents over time, they would constitute a further significant step in assuring a successful security system not dependent on nuclear weapons. Of course, appropriate precautions would have to be taken to guard the guardians.

6.   *Create a permanent international criminal court* with compulsory jurisdiction specifically over war crimes, crimes against the peace, and crimes against humanity, accessible by multilateral intergovernmental organizations, nongovernmental entities, and qualified individuals, as well as by States.[31]

In addition to these six institutional initiatives one should mention, of course, the need to reform the United Nations, particularly in relation to the antiquated anachronistic composition of the Security Council, which has primary responsibility for the maintenance of international peace and security. The failure so far to ensure more equitable Third World representation among the Council's permanent members (in the name, say, of Brazil, Egypt, Indonesia, or Nigeria), plus the absence among the permanent members of economically powerful Germany and Japan, raise fundamental questions about the determination and orchestration, not to mention the moral premise, of the U.N.'s peace and security operations. Antinuclear activists should take this issue seriously and try to do something about it.

THUS, a number of possible policy initiatives to which dedicated peace activists, lawyers and non-lawyers alike, may commit themselves. It bears emphasis, however, that all of the above recommendations are the logical outgrowth of a lexicology that defines non-nuclear security—personal, national, and international—almost exclusively in terms of the absence of war or the threat of war. As a consequence, they bespeak the norms, procedures, and institutions that facilitate the prevention or elimination of military confrontation and conflict. And yet, as became increasingly clear from the worldwide economic and environmental pressures of the 1970s and 1980s, a definition of security informed preeminently by concern for military risks and encounters is not adequately responsive to the full range of threats to our personal, national, and international security that we now encounter and are likely to encounter in the 1990s and the years after 2000 as well.

In other words, achieving true global security will require not only a drastic circumscription of nuclear and, more generally, militarist tendencies, but also the progressive development of those norms, procedures, and institutions that can assist the promotion and protection of social justice, economic well-being, and ecological balance on a worldwide scale. It is social injustice, economic malaise, and environmental decline that lead, independently and interdependently, to frustration, conflict, and oftentimes violence. The evidence is all around us. Therefore, a non-nuclear global security system is unlikely to succeed if it is not marked also by a broad and deep commitment to the widespread realization of fundamental human rights and freedoms, to the wholesale eradication of grinding poverty and economic dependency, and to the unwavering stewardship of our earth-space environment as a total living organism, meant to be cherished rather than squandered. To these ends, of course, including the repeal of the parochial, piecemeal, and timorous policies that have allowed ours to become a seriously endangered planet, there is vast room for law, lawyering, and political action, both domestic and international.

And the moment for acting seems ripe. For the first time in more than forty-five years, a serious revived interest in normative, procedural, and structural change has emerged on the global plane. The profound and profoundly exhilarating events of the last several years, brought about in part by *glasnost* and *perestroika*, attest to this development: the ending of the Cold War and the accompanying disengagement of East-West military forces; the democratization of Eastern Europe; the heightened integration of Western Europe come 1992 and the credible possibility of some all-European unity sometime thereafter; the unification of the two Germanies; the Gorbachev embrace of international law; the rollback of apartheid in Namibia and the beginning of its eradication in South Africa; the reemergence of the United Nations; and so forth. Separately, as well as together, these events lead one to appreciate that "reality" is never fixed and that the magnitude of the struggle for world peace is not so overwhelming as to be beyond human capacity.

I.

The Opinions of Judges Boyle, Rubin and Weston

Federation of Earth

Provisional District World Court

Los Angeles, California, U.S.A.

In re:

MORE THAN 50,000 NUCLEAR WEAPONS

THE PEOPLE OF THE EARTH,

PLAINTIFFS,

-vs-

CHINA (PEOPLE'S REPUBLIC), FRANCE, UNION OF SO-
VIET SOCIALIST REPS., UNITED KINGDOM, UNITED
STATES, BELGIUM, BULGARIA, CANADA, CZECHOSLO-
VAKIA, GERMAN DEM. REP., FED. REP. OF GERMANY,
GREECE, HUNGARY, ITALY, NETHERLANDS, POLAND,
ROMANIA, SOUTH KOREA, SPAIN, TAIWAN, ARGENTINA,
BRAZIL, INDIA, IRAQ, ISRAEL, LIBYA, PAKISTAN, SOUTH
AFRICA,

DEFENDANTS.

PDWC NO. LA-83-0001

JUDGMENT

Boyle, Rubin and Weston, JJ.

This case has been brought in the Provisional District World Court of the Federation of Earth by the People of the Earth organized under the Constitution of the Federation of Earth. Plaintiffs pray this Court to declare that nuclear weapons are illegal under international and world law, and ask this Court to issue a permanent injunction prohibiting the design, research, testing, production, manufacture, fabrication, transportation, deployment, installation, maintaining, storing, stockpiling, sale, purchase as well as the use or threatened use of any nuclear weapons by any country or any person or persons. At a public hearing in Los Angeles, California, U.S.A., Federation of Earth, on January 17, 1987, oral arguments were presented to Judges Boyle, Rubin and Weston supported by elaborate written submissions by Plaintiffs and Counsel representing Defendants in absentia under the laws of the Federation of Earth. Judges Boyle, Rubin and Weston heard all the arguments and examined all the briefs and supplemental materials properly presented, and have consulted together. They conclude that this tribunal has the necessary jurisdiction but find their different approaches to questions of substance make a collective decision more likely to confuse than to clarify the legal issues each believes to be significant. Thus, while there is a coincident conclusion that at least some uses of nuclear weapons should be forbidden by injunction, the argumentation that might be used to find that the law places further restrictions on the rights of states to arm themselves is stated in three different opinions. The areas of concurrence being small, and the areas of inconsistent argumentation being great, those are separate, not concurring, opinions.

Jurisdiction in this Court rests upon the Constitution of the Federation of Earth. Failure of the Defendants to recognize the existence of the Federation and legal force of its Constitution is irrelevant to the issue, which is one of Federation law. If Federation law is inconsistent with public international law, that seems a matter for the political arms of the Federation Government, and not for a Court established under the Constitution of the Federation. This is the position taken by national tribunals of many states with similar Constitutions to that of the Federation.

We therefore hold that there is jurisdiction in this Court to hear the case under the law of the Federation of Earth.

As to substance, we refer to our separate opinions.

DATED: July 1, 1988

Francis A. Boyle
Alfred P. Rubin
Burns H. Weston

Judges,
Provisional District World Court
Federation of Earth

SEPARATE OPINION BY FRANCIS A. BOYLE

Introduction

1.   The human race stands on the verge of self-extinction as a species, and with it will die most if not all forms of intelligent life on the planet earth. In the hope of preventing a nuclear Armageddon, the jurists of the world must come together to proclaim certain fundamental principles concerning the requirements of international law with respect to nuclear weapons. It is my hope that the following analysis will serve to define in legal terms the stark dilemma of nuclear extinction that confronts the human race today. It also seeks to establish an agenda for other jurists around the world to pursue by applying their unique training, skills, and expertise in a productive and meaningful way toward the progressive yet complete elimination of nuclear weapons from the face of the earth. Realistically speaking, we cannot expect this to happen in the immediate future. Nevertheless, jurists owe a special obligation to our fellow men and women around the world to struggle toward this goal with all the powers of our profession. It is for these reasons, then, that I have decided to write a Separate Opinion in this case.

Hiroshima and Nagasaki

2.   Any attempt to dispel the ideology of nuclearism and its attendant myth propounding the legality of nuclear weapons must directly come to grips with the fact that the nuclear age was conceived in the original sins of Hiroshima and Nagasaki on August 6 and 9, 1945. The atomic bombings of Hiroshima and Nagasaki constituted crimes against humanity and war crimes as defined by the Nuremberg Charter of August 8, 1945, and violated several basic provisions of the Regulations annexed to Hague Convention No. IV Respecting the Laws and Customs of War on Land (1907), the rules of customary international law set forth in the Draft Hague Rules of Air Warfare (1923), and the United States War Department Field Manual 27-10, Rules of Land Warfare (1940). According to this Field Manual and the principles of the Nuremberg Charter, all civilian government

officials and military officers who ordered or knowingly partici-
pated in the atomic bombings of Hiroshima and Nagasaki could
have been (and still can be) lawfully punished as war criminals.
The start of any progress toward resolving humankind's nuclear
predicament must come from the realization that nuclear weapons have never been legitimate instruments of state policy, but
rather have always constituted illegitimate instrumentalities of
internationally lawless and criminal behavior.

The Use of Nuclear Weapons

3.   The use of nuclear weapons in combat is absolutely
prohibited under all circumstances by both conventional and
customary international law: e.g., the Nuremberg Principles,
the Hague Regulations of 1907, the International Convention on
the Prevention and Punishment of the Crime of Genocide of
1948, the Four Geneva Conventions of 1949 and their Additional
Protocol I of 1977, etc. In addition, the use of nuclear weapons
would also specifically violate several fundamental resolutions
of the United Nations General Assembly that have repeatedly
condemned the use of nuclear weapons as an international
crime. For example, on November 24, 1961, the U.N. General
Assembly declared in Resolution 1653 (XVI) that "any State
using nuclear or thermonuclear weapons is to be considered as
violating the Charter of the United Nations, as acting contrary
to the law of humanity, and as committing a crime against
mankind and civilization." In Resolution 33/71-B of December
14, 1978 and Resolution 35/152-D of December 12, 1980, the
General Assembly again declared that "the use of nuclear weapons would be a violation of the Charter of the United Nations and
a crime against humanity." Finally, the International Peace
Bureau's Appeal by Lawyers Against Nuclear War (1986)—
which has already been endorsed by thousands of lawyers
around the world—declared that "the use, for whatever reason,
of a nuclear weapon would constitute (a) a violation of international law, (b) a violation of human rights, and (c) a crime against
humanity."

Nuremberg Responsibility

4.   As jurists, we are compelled by the Nuremberg Principles to point out the following inescapable conclusions of law to all government decision-makers in the nuclear weapons states: First, according to the Nuremberg Judgment, soldiers would be obliged to disobey egregiously illegal orders with respect to launching and waging a nuclear war. Second, all government officials and military officers who might nevertheless launch or wage a nuclear war would be personally responsible for the commission of crimes against peace, crimes against humanity, war crimes, grave breaches of the Geneva Conventions and Protocol I, and genocide, among other international crimes. Third, such individuals would not be entitled to the defenses of superior orders, act of state, *tu quoque*, self-defense, etc. Fourth, such individuals could thus be quite legitimately and most severely punished as war criminals, up to and including the imposition of the death penalty.

5.   Under article 38(1)(d) of the Statute of the International Court of Justice, this Opinion constitutes a "subsidiary means for the determination of rules of law." It could therefore be relied upon by some future international war crimes tribunal. As jurists, however, our primary concern must be to prevent a nuclear war from ever happening.

The Threat to Use Nuclear Weapons

6.   Article 2(4) of the United Nations Charter of 1945 prohibits both the threat and the use of force except in cases of legitimate self-defense as recognized by article 51 thereof. But although the requirement of legitimate self-defense is a necessary precondition for the legality of any threat or use of force, it is certainly not sufficient. For the legality of any threat or use of force must also take into account the customary and conventional international laws of humanitarian armed conflict.

7.   Thereunder, the threat to use nuclear weapons (i.e., nuclear deterrence/terrorism) constitutes ongoing international criminal activity: Namely, planning, preparation, solicitation and conspiracy to commit crimes against peace, crimes against humanity, war crimes, genocide, as well as grave breaches of the

Four Geneva Conventions of 1949, Additional Protocol I of 1977, the Hague Regulations of 1907, and the International Convention on the Prevention and Punishment of the Crime of Genocide of 1948, *inter alia*. These are the so-called inchoate crimes that under the Nuremberg Principles constitute international crimes in their own right.

8.   The conclusion is inexorable, therefore, that the design, research, testing, production, manufacture, fabrication, transportation, deployment, installation, maintenance, storing, stockpiling, sale, and purchase as well as the threat to use nuclear weapons together with all their essential accouterments are criminal under well-recognized principles of international law. Thus, those government decision-makers in the nuclear weapons states with command responsibility for their nuclear weapons establishments are today subject to personal criminal responsibility under the Nuremberg Principles for this criminal practice of nuclear deterrence/terrorism that they have daily inflicted upon all states and peoples of the international community. Here I wish to single out four components of the threat to use nuclear weapons that are especially reprehensible from an international law perspective: counter-ethnic targeting; counter-city targeting; first-strike weapons and contingency plans; and the first-use of nuclear weapons to repel a conventional attack.

Counter-Ethnic Targeting

9.   It has been reported that various government officials in some nuclear weapons states have supervised the construction of war-plans for the threat and use of nuclear weapons systems that incorporate a philosophy known as "counter-ethnic targeting." In other words, major population centers inhabited primarily by members of certain ethnic groups were selected for repeated and especially severe nuclear destruction because of their constituent ethnicity alone. Whatever the alleged political justification for this practice, all government officials who were involved in the nuclear targeting of ethnic groups as such actually committed the international crime of conspiracy to commit genocide, as recognized by articles 1, 2, 3 and 4 of the 1948 Genocide Convention.

Counter-City Targeting

10. A nuclear attack by a state upon another state's civilian population centers is absolutely prohibited under all circumstances, even if undertaken in retaliation for a prior nuclear attack against the first state's civilian population centers. Consequently, the doctrine of "mutual assured destruction" (MAD) must be abandoned as an element of any strategic nuclear deterrence/terrorist policy currently pursued by the nuclear weapons states. Nevertheless, any plan to substitute for MAD the development of a "protracted nuclear war-fighting" or "war-prevailing" capability is not a licit direction in which to move under international law. Rather, the correct approach is prescribed by article 6 of the 1968 Treaty on the Non-Proliferation of Nuclear Weapons (NPT), which the United States, the Soviet Union and the United Kingdom are strictly bound to obey as parties: "Each of the Parties to the Treaty undertakes to pursue negotiations in good faith on effective measures relating to cessation of the nuclear arms race at an early date and to nuclear disarmament, and on a treaty on general and complete disarmament under strict and effective international control." In regard to the achievement of this latter objective, we must emphasize the continued utility of the U.S.-U.S.S.R. Joint Statement of Agreed Principles for Disarmament Negotiations of 20 September 1961, the so-called McCloy-Zorin Accords.

11. In the meantime, however, while moving toward the goals set forth in NPT article 6, the nuclear weapons states are obligated to recognize and declare that in the event of a nuclear or conventional attack upon them or the members of their respective alliances, they could not under any circumstances actually use their nuclear weapons against civilian population centers. Although this is already the legal situation, we must call for the nuclear weapons states immediately to conclude an international convention specifically prohibiting both a nuclear attack upon, as well as the strategic nuclear targeting of, civilian population centers. This treaty would then need to be implemented by the nuclear weapons states' respective national parliaments making it a serious criminal offense under domestic law for their government officials or military officers to threaten or plan to use nuclear weapons against civilian population centers.

First-Strike Weapons and Contingency Plans

12. A surprise, preemptive nuclear strike by one country against another would be a crime against peace and therefore is absolutely prohibited for any reason whatsoever. Consequently, all first-strike strategic nuclear weapons as well as their concomitant command, control and communications systems and first-strike contingency plans and practice scenarios are prohibited, illegal, and criminal. In order to strengthen that prohibition, we must call for the nuclear weapons states to conclude a treaty that (1) prohibits the further deployment of first-strike nuclear weapons systems, (2) requires the destruction of those already deployed, and (3) mandates the removal of all first-strike contingency scenarios from governmental war-plans.

13. Pursuant thereto, the nuclear weapons states' respective national parliaments must pass implementing legislation making it a serious criminal offense under domestic law for government officials and military officers to design or practice first-strike scenarios during war games or otherwise. These developments would facilitate the conclusion of an international convention specifically prohibiting the nuclear weapons states from adopting a "launch-on-warning" nuclear response doctrine as well as all forms of command, control and communications systems supportive thereof and any forms of testing incidental thereto. Such measures would, hopefully, lessen the likelihood of any nuclear weapons state feeling compelled by the circumstance of a severe international crisis to seriously consider being the first to resort to the use of nuclear weapons.

The First-Use of Nuclear Weapons

14. Furthermore, the first-use of nuclear weapons to repel a conventional attack would be totally disproportionate and indiscriminate to the threat presented and therefore constitute an impermissible act of self-defense. Therefore, both NATO and the Warsaw Pact must phase out all of their battlefield, short-range and theater nuclear weapons systems from Europe as part of a mutually negotiated process. In this regard, we must applaud the efforts by the United States and the Soviet Union to eliminate so-called theater or intermediate range nuclear

weapons systems deployed on that continent by means of the December 1987 INF Treaty. We must also encourage them to initiate negotiations over the elimination of all so-called battlefield nuclear weapons from Europe. The immediate and complete denuclearization of Europe by the respective members of NATO and the Warsaw Pact is a political, legal, and moral imperative.

15. The Soviet Union and China have each already given a unilateral pledge of "no-first-use" of nuclear weapons that creates a binding international legal obligation on its own accord. The United States and the concerned NATO members must respond in kind by doing the same, and then expressing their readiness to conclude an international convention to that effect with the members of the Warsaw Pact. Considerations of international law would fully support such a "no-first-use" treaty as a preliminary step toward the complete denuclearization of Europe. Other nuclear weapons states could then join this convention for the purpose of initiating a denuclearization of their respective regions in the world. However, we must emphatically reject the notion that the denuclearization of Europe will require the increased conventional militarization of that continent.

16. Such negotiations for the complete denuclearization of Europe could be tied into the successor to the Mutual and Balanced Force Reduction (MBFR) negotiations, which had been taking place at Vienna. In the proposals on the table there, both sides were in basic agreement on the principle that NATO and the Warsaw Pact should each reduce to the identical level of 900,000 men, with no more than 700,000 ground troops. The achievement of a rough equality in conventional forces at such lower levels between NATO and the Warsaw Pact would materially reduce any incentive for either to launch a conventional attack while at the same time it would obviate the need for a massive buildup in European conventional forces. In this manner, an effective conventional deterrent could be maintained at lower levels of potential violence on both sides without the need for either to field an alleged nuclear deterrent to a conventional attack.

The Criminality of Nuclear Weapons

17.   As can be determined in part from the preceding analysis, today's nuclear weapons establishments as well as the entire system of nuclear deterrence/terrorism currently practiced by the nuclear weapon states are criminal—not simply illegal, not simply immoral, but criminal under well-recognized principles of international law. This simple idea of the criminality of nuclear weapons can be utilized to pierce through the ideology of nuclearism to which many citizens in the nuclear weapons states have succumbed. It is with this simple idea of the criminality of nuclear weapons that such people can proceed to comprehend the inherent illegitimacy and fundamental lawlessness of the policies that their governments pursue in their names with respect to the further development of nuclear weapons systems.

18.   The idea of the criminality of nuclear weapons is quite simple. And yet simple ideas are oftentimes the most powerful. For example, at one point in historical time, people saw no problem with the institution of slavery. But as a result of the Abolitionist Movement in England and the United States, the entire international community eventually came around to the point of view that slavery and the slave trade were immoral, illegal, and criminal and therefore must be abolished and re-pressed, which they were and still are today. The same type of moral and perceptual transformation must occur now with respect to nuclear weapons in those states that possess them.

19.   In all fairness, however, I should point out that there are today tens of thousands of people in the United States of America who truly believe that nuclear weapons are criminal under well-recognized principles of international law that have been fully subscribed to by the United States government and incorporated into United States domestic law. That number is increasing every day. Furthermore, there are hundreds of thousands of people in Europe who believe that nuclear weapons systems are criminal, and that number is increasing every day. Finally, there are tens of millions of people around the world who believe that nuclear weapons systems are criminal. It therefore becomes necessary for all of us to further propagate the idea of the criminality of nuclear weapons in order to increase the number of people who hold that opinion here in the United

States as well as in the other nuclear weapons states for the purpose of compelling them to consider developing constructive strategies for the abolition of nuclear weapons from the face of the earth.

The Right of Anti-Nuclear Civil Resistance

20. In light of the fact that nuclear weapons systems are prohibited, illegal, and criminal under all circumstances and for any reason, every person around the world possesses a basic human right to be free from this criminal practice of nuclear deterrence/terrorism and its concomitant specter of nuclear extinction. Thus, all human beings possess the basic right under international law to engage in non-violent civil resistance activities for the purpose of preventing or terminating the ongoing commission of these international crimes. Every citizen of the world community has both the right and the duty to oppose the existence of nuclear weapons systems by whatever non-violent means are at his or her disposal.

World Opinion Juris

21. Humankind must abolish nuclear weapons before nuclear weapons abolish humankind. Nonetheless, a small number of governments in the world community continue to maintain nuclear weapons systems despite the rules of international criminal law to the contrary. This has led some international lawyers to argue that since there exist a few nuclear weapons states in the world community, therefore nuclear weapons must somehow not be criminal because otherwise these few states would not possess nuclear weapons systems. In other words, to use lawyers' parlance, this minority state practice of nuclear deterrence/terrorism by the great powers somehow negates the existence of a world opinion juris (i.e., sense of legal obligation) as to the criminality of nuclear weapons.

22. There is a very simple response to that tautological argument: Since when has a small gang of criminals—in this case, the nuclear weapons states—been able to determine what is legal or illegal for the rest of the community by means of their

own criminal behavior? What right do these nuclear weapons states have to argue that by means of their own criminal behavior they have *ipso facto* made criminal acts legitimate? No civilized nation state would permit a small gang of criminal conspirators to pervert its domestic legal order in this manner. Moreover, both the Nuremberg Tribunal and the Tokyo Tribunal made it quite clear that a conspiratorial band of criminal states likewise has no right to opt out of the international legal order by means of invoking their own criminal behavior as the least common denominator of international deportment.

The Criminal Conspiracy of Nuclear Deterrence/Terrorism

23. To the contrary, the entire human race has been victimized by an international conspiracy of ongoing criminal activity carried out by the nuclear weapons states under the doctrine known as "nuclear deterrence," which is a euphemism for "nuclear terrorism." This international conspiracy of nuclear deterrence/terrorism currently practiced by the nuclear weapons states is no different from any other conspiracy by a criminal gang or band. They are the outlaws. So it is up to the rest of the international community to repress and dissolve this international criminal conspiracy as soon as possible and by whatever non-violent means are available.

24.   Here in the United States, there are several ramifications that follow ineluctably from the conspiratorial doctrine and practice known as nuclear deterrence/terrorism. First, criminality is said to be legitimacy. When nuclear weapons were first developed and used, there was absolutely no consideration given to the rule of law. Thus, nuclear weapons represent the absolute negation of a rule of law both at home and abroad. The very existence of nuclear weapons requires that the rule of law be subverted both at home and abroad.

25. Furthermore, nuclear weapons are anti-democratic. There has never been any form of meaningful democratic accountability applied to the U.S. nuclear weapons establishment. The American people as individuals or as a whole have never had any significant input into the process of developing nuclear weapons systems except to the extent that Congress has voted

blank checks. The very existence of nuclear weapons systems and their requisite degrees of super-secrecy require that our system of government be stealthily anti-democratic.

26. Finally, the same is true for the Constitution. Constitutional protections became meaningless when nuclear weapons were integrated into the U.S. foreign affairs and defense establishment. Indeed, the U.S. Constitution has become a farce and a facade in the name of national security as a direct result of nuclear weapons. In a similar manner, fundamental principles of legality, democracy, and constitutionality have been trampled under foot by all the nuclear weapons states in their mad stampede toward humankind's nuclear abyss.

The Irrationality of Irrationality

27. Nuclear deterrence/terrorism as currently practiced by today's nuclear weapons states—this small gang of international criminal conspirators—cannot succeed over the long run because it is premised upon assumptions and practices that are immoral, illegal, unconstitutional, criminal, and irrational in the estimation of the respective public opinions in the various nuclear weapons states as well as around the world. Unless it is destroyed, nuclear deterrence/terrorism will ultimately fail and destroy all of humankind because of its own inherent contradictions. In particular, the assumptions, policies, and practices underlying the U.S. nuclear weapons establishment are irrational and insane from any meaningful perspective. Nevertheless, this conspiratorial doctrine of nuclear deterrence/terrorism has required that what is inherently irrational and insane somehow be made to appear to be completely rational and sane. America has quite necessarily had to invert and pervert its entire system of democratic values, legal ethos, and constitutional practices in order to account for and accommodate the existence of nuclear weapons.

28. For example, a good deal of the U.S. nuclear weapons establishment and deterrence/terrorist practices are premised upon the Harvard political scientist Thomas Schelling's theory known as the "rationality of irrationality" that was expounded in his classic book *The Strategy of Conflict* (1960). According to this pernicious doctrine, in theory it could sometimes prove to be a

rational strategy for a government decision-maker to pretend to be completely irrational in his dealings with other states in order to get his own way. Adolph Hitler was the paradigmatic example of this phenomenon during the 1930s. The outbreak of the Second World War in 1939, however, demonstrated the limitations of this theory.

29. Applying Schelling's concept to nuclear weapons, an analyst could mistakenly come to the conclusion that it might prove to be useful for a government to threaten to commit the completely irrational and insane act of starting a nuclear war in order to avoid a conventional or nuclear war, or more cynically and realistically, to achieve certain geopolitical objectives. Furthermore, in order to make this insane threat credible, the threatening state must then supposedly proceed to develop the capability to launch and wage a nuclear war so that in the eyes of its intended adversary the completely irrational threat might begin to look somewhat more rational. When the adversary inevitably responds in kind, these psychological and bureaucratic dynamics produce the momentum for generating the self-fulfilling prophecy of nuclear Armageddon.

30. I will not bother here to analyze at any length the logical contradictions and psychological fallacies of U.S. nuclear deterrence\terrorist doctrine since that task has already been performed quite admirably by Robert Jervis in his definitive work *The Illogic of American Nuclear Strategy* (1984). But I simply wish to point out that the entire theory of nuclear deterrence/terrorism as currently practiced by the world's nuclear weapons states represents a working-out of Schelling's hypothesis propounding the "rationality of irrationality." All of the world's nuclear weapons states, and especially the two nuclear superpowers, have spent the past forty-five years trying to make a completely irrational threat appear to be rational and in the process have had to pervert and destroy all elements of rationality, legality, constitutionality, morality, and sanity that stood in their way. The task itself is ultimately doomed to failure unless and until the citizens of the world's nuclear weapons states can figure out some practical means to eliminate nuclear weapons before nuclear weapons eliminate them.

The Illegal Status of Nuclear Arms Control Agreements

31.   These observations then logically bring us to the question of the international legal status of nuclear arms control agreements.   From the perspective developed above, nuclear arms control agreements are simply part of an international criminal conspiracy between a small gang of criminal states designed to further perpetuate the conspiracy. Nuclear arms control agreements attempt to rationalize, regularize, modernize, and perfect the instrumentalities of international criminal activity. Hence, they are entitled to no validity at all as a matter of positive international law.

32.   Nevertheless, until humankind can get rid of those instrumentalities of crime, it is probably preferable to try to control nuclear weapons than not to try to control them. To be sure, a good argument can be made that nuclear arms control negotiations have never constituted more than soporifics designed by the nuclear weapons states, and especially by the two superpowers, to lull world public opinion into a false sense of trust in the process while, under their deceptive guise, these governments have pursued an unrelenting nuclear arms buildup. Yet, whatever position one ultimately takes on this issue, we must never forget that all forms of nuclear arms control treaties concluded between the United States and the Soviet Union and among the nuclear weapons states themselves still deal with the instrumentalities of internationally criminal and lawless behavior.

33. Thus, nuclear arms control agreements can only constitute a temporary expedient. Their overall objective must always remain that prescribed by article 6 of the 1968 Treaty on the Non-Proliferation of Nuclear Weapons. To reiterate: "Each of the Parties to the Treaty undertakes to pursue negotiations in good faith on effective measures relating to cessation of the nuclear arms race at an early date and to nuclear disarmament, and on a treaty on general and complete disarmament under strict and effective international control." Universal nuclear disarmament is the only legally defensible, morally acceptable, and logically consistent position that can be taken.

Strategic Arms Reduction Agreements

34. That being said, the May 1986 decision by the Reagan administration to repudiate the 1972 SALT I Interim Agreement freezing the number of ballistic missile launchers and the SALT II Treaty of 1979 was especially shortsighted. If any new strategic arms reduction agreement is to be reached between the United States and the Soviet Union, it will have to be based upon the fundamentals of the SALT I and SALT II Treaties. Strategic arms reductions could occur by both parties agreeing to modify a revised SALT II by means of lowering its numerical limitations on strategic nuclear delivery vehicle launchers and its sublimitations on multiple independently targetable reentry vehicles (MIRVs) by fifty percent (50%) over a period of five years. Next, it would then be possible for these two nuclear weapons states to create a formal mechanism that would mandate a percentage reduction in the SALT I and SALT II limitations on launchers and sublimitations on MIRVed systems on a periodic basis (e.g., 5-10% per annum). The implementation of such a procedure must be designed to result in the complete elimination of strategic nuclear weapons systems in the foreseeable future and by a date-certain (e.g., the year 2000 A.D.).

The Strategic Defense Initiative

35. Unfortunately, the prospects for genuine strategic nuclear arms reductions have been seriously set back by the Reagan administration's proclamation of the so-called Strategic Defense Initiative (SDI) in 1983. That act represented nothing less than a formal statement by the United States government of its intention to pursue a policy that will eventually result in the commission of numerous material breaches of the 1972 U.S.-U.S.S.R. Anti-Ballistic Missile Systems (ABM) Treaty. In other words, the SDI program actually constitutes an anticipatory repudiation of the ABM Treaty itself. In addition, SDI would probably violate the 1967 Outer Space Treaty, which prohibits the deployment of some of SDI's envisioned weapons of mass destruction in outer space. Moreover, field testing some of SDI's proposed technologies (e.g., the x-ray laser) would violate the pathbreaking 1963 Limited Test Ban Treaty, which specifically

prohibits any type of nuclear explosion in outer space.

36. We must call upon the United States government to reaffirm its commitment to the clear language as well as to its longstanding interpretation of the ABM Treaty, and, therefore, to immediately terminate the SDI program. Furthermore, the ABM Treaty must be strengthened by the conclusion of a separate international convention that prohibits the development, testing, and deployment of anti-satellite weapons systems, which can also be used for SDI purposes. Finally, the U.S. and the U.S.S.R. must clarify the limited scope of permissible "research" under the ABM Treaty by means of concluding a supplementary protocol for that purpose.

Nuclear Free Zones

37. Significant progress by the two superpowers in the areas of reducing strategic nuclear weapons and preventing space weapons can facilitate the complete elimination of nuclear weapons systems at the regional level. In this regard, we must commend the efforts by governments, statesmen, and private individuals around the world to establish so-called "nuclear-free zones" in Europe, Latin America, and the South Pacific, etc. It would also be a positive development to establish nuclear-free zones at the national, state, and local levels as well. In addition, building upon existing treaties, the nuclear-free-zone principle should be applied on a permanent and universal basis to Outer Space, Antarctica, the Deep Seabed, the Arctic Ocean, the Indian Ocean, Africa, and the Middle East, *inter alia*. The progressive development of the nuclear-free-zone movement has the potential to close-off large sections of the global commons to the criminal activities by the nuclear weapons states and to the further proliferation of nuclear weapons.

Comprehensive Test Ban Treaty

38. The decision by the Reagan administration to reject the invitation by the Soviet government to duplicate its imposition of a unilateral moratorium on the underground testing of nuclear weapons upon the occasion of the fortieth anniversary of the

atomic bombing of Hiroshima was deplorable. Under the afore-mentioned principles of international law, all of the nuclear weapons states are obligated to impose an immediate morato-rium on the design, testing, development, deployment, and modernization of all forms of nuclear weapons and their atten-dant delivery and communications systems. Those concerned nuclear weapons states must also return to the negotiations for the conclusion of a Comprehensive Test Ban Treaty (CTBT), which were unilaterally suspended by the United States govern-ment in 1980. The successful conclusion of a CTBT under strict national and international verification would serve as a signifi-cant impediment to the faster acceleration of the nuclear arms race as well as to the further proliferation of nuclear weapons around the world.

Nuclear Proliferation

39. To a significant extent, the proliferation of nuclear weapons and the capability to produce them can be directly attributable to the failure of the concerned nuclear weapons states, and especially the two superpowers, "to pursue negotiations in good faith on effective measures relating to cessation of the nuclear arms race at an early date and to nuclear disarmament ..." as required by article 6 of the 1968 Nuclear Non-Proliferation Treaty. We must call upon the concerned nuclear weapons states to strictly discharge their solemn obligations under NPT article 6. We must also urge those acknowledged nuclear weapons states that have not yet accepted the NPT to become parties. Finally, we must encourage those states which possess the capability to construct nuclear weapons but have not yet accepted the NPT to become parties and thereby expressly renounce any nuclear intentions. The security of states is fatally threatened, not protected, by the acquisition or development of a nuclear weapons capability. In addition to joining the NPT regime, the security of non-nuclear weapons states in various regions around the world can best be promoted by means of the mechanisms envisioned by Chapter VIII of the United Nations Charter on Regional Arrangements.

The Rule of International Law

40. We must reaffirm our unswerving commitment to the rule of international law, to the peaceful settlement of international disputes, to upholding the integrity of the United Nations Organization, and to respecting the authority of the International Court of Justice. Pursuant to this commitment, we must urge the membership of the U.N. General Assembly to give serious consideration to the conclusion of an international convention that expressly criminalizes the possession, design, testing, development, manufacture, deployment, use, and the threat to use "nuclear weapons" specifically by that name. Moreover, the General Assembly must give urgent consideration to further steps that would lead to the complete elimination of nuclear weapons from the face of the earth. In particular, the General Assembly should request an Advisory Opinion from the International Court of Justice on the general subject of Nuclear Weapons and International Law. A sound repudiation of the alleged legality of the threat or use of nuclear weapons and of the nuclear arms race by the International Court of Justice would go a long way toward convincing the entire international community that nuclear weapons are not legitimate instruments of state policy, but rather manifestations of lawlessness and criminality.

Conclusion

41. Admittedly, the agenda set forth above is ambitious, but under the specter of nuclear extinction, we have no alternative but to struggle for its achievement. We must call upon all jurists and lawyers' organizations around the world, as well as all men and women of good faith everywhere, to join us in this crusade for universal nuclear disarmament. Otherwise, the human race will suffer the same fate as the dinosaurs, and the planet earth will become a radioactive wasteland. The time for preventive action is now! Consequently, I would grant the injunctive relief as requested in full by plaintiffs, The People of the Earth.

DATED: June 6, 1988

Francis A. Boyle
Judge, Provisional District, World Court

SEPARATE OPINION OF ALFRED P. RUBIN

The possession of nuclear weapons is clearly forbidden by the Constitution of the Federation of Earth. But the terms of this proceeding under that Constitution contain a choice of law referral to public international law or "world law." Under the Constitution, we are free to accept that choice of law referral, and I do so.

In discussing public international law, it is first necessary in my opinion to distinguish between that law as a legal order *strictu sensu* and morality. Rules of international society, like the rules of particular states within international society, are not identical with the ethical or moral principles that govern society on a deeper level. Nor are the rules of law or the rules of morality identical with the rules of expedient policy. The distinctions among the sources, applications, and enforcement techniques of these different sets of rules is the subject of libraries of learned writing and not capable of being set out simply in this place. But a certain preliminary discussion is necessary in order that my opinion be made comprehensible.

In the following discussion, for simplicity, "possession" will be used to include all the possible synonyms for possession and all activities leading to possession and all activities except "use" or threat of "use." Since the ability to dispose of nuclear weapons is necessary for the use or threat of use to be real, "possession" will in this opinion include that ability even if actual physical custody of the weapons is elsewhere. Thus "possession" in this opinion will include all the words used in the prayer for injunctive relief other than "use". "Use" will include all the military uses of nuclear energy for purposes of destruction or imposing will, including the mere "threat" of use, which cannot be effective unless believed, even if the "threat" or "use" would be consistent with Articles 2(4) or 51 of the Charter of the United Nations. The only sense in which use is not included in this opinion is use for peaceful power production consistent with arrangements envisaged by the International Atomic Energy Agency.

A. Morality, Law, and Policy

Moralists, using their own definitions and traditions, can discuss whether the possession or use of nuclear weapons is consistent with morality.[1] Policy planners, frequently regarding morals as irrelevant to their "realism," can also discuss whether the possession or use of nuclear weapons is sufficiently important to the national interest to warrant the expenditure of funds and the exercise of political will necessary for research, development, and deployment. International lawyers have their own traditions, which reflect those moral perceptions that statesmen actually act by, whether consciously or not, and those policy decisions that have become the subject of international correspondence or controversy.

The bridge over which moral considerations move to become binding on a country and cease to be matters about which people can actively disagree in principle is the "legislative" process.[2] Moral consideration and practical political experience are translated by this process into rules that are regarded by wise political leaders as "law" and therefore binding as a limit on policy choices. Public international law includes rules about making rules; it has a legislative process through which moral rules and notions of political expediency can become binding as substantive rules of behavior restricting the discretion of states, and thus of political leaders acting in their official capacities. Failure to obey these substantive rules is not "criminal" activity subject to punishment by "police" action, but it can lead a state into "tortious" activity with "damages," reprisals, and various forms of decentralized or, in some cases, coordinated community reactions being the legal result. It can destroy the fabric of international society creating a world of each against all which people have struggled to rise out of since the dawn of civilization. In this sense, violation of the substantive rules of public international law, even for apparent political advantage, can never be politically wise.

B. Possession of Nuclear Weapons

Applying the methods of legal thought to the question of whether possession of nuclear weapons is permissible first requires that purely moral arguments against the possession of the means to do evil must be put aside. Similarly, purely political arguments about the desirability of possessing the weapons in order to increase national prestige or influence must be put aside. Also, combined political-moral arguments resting on the assumption that retaliation in kind is part of the enforcement process of public international law presume that the use of the weapons is illegal, and must be put aside until that prior question is answered; thus the political argument that possession of nuclear weapons must be permissible to enable a state to deter their use by others, or the moral argument that possession must be permissible to enable a state to take revenge against prior use by others in the exercise of what might be called "retributive justice," are irrelevant to the strictly legal question, however compelling those arguments might seem to some politicians and moralists.

From the point of view of public international law, there seem to be two major arguments against the legality of mere possession of nuclear weapons. The first argument stems from the increasing number of treaties and proposals for treaties favoring nuclear-free zones and non-proliferation of nuclear weapons, which might reflect a growing consensus among political leaders against such possession. The second argument rests on analogies and inferences drawn from existing prohibitions on certain non-nuclear weapons, prohibitions supported by treaties and probably by general international law as well. If the possession of weapons less discriminate or destructive than nuclear weapons is already forbidden by law, then *a fortiori* the possession of nuclear weapons might be considered to be included in the lesser prohibition.

As to the first argument, the general expansion of nuclear-free zone and non-proliferation agreements, there seems to be ample evidence that whatever other motives might be involved, treaties creating nuclear-free zones, like the Treaty of Tlatelolco, signed on 14 February 1967,[3] reflect less a rejection of the legality of possessing nuclear weapons than a reluctance to have them possessed in particular places that statesmen have concluded could be defended better by other means. Similarly, the Antarctic Treaty of 1959 prohibits all military bases and the testing of any weapons in the treaty area.[4] Nuclear explosions and the disposal of radioactive wastes in the Antarctic are expressly forbidden, but these terms do not prohibit the possession of nuclear weapons as such. There is no clear evidence that the policy of de-nuclearizing the Antarctic reflects any sense that possessing nuclear weapons is illegal.

The Nuclear Non-Proliferation Treaty of 1 July 1968 does not purport to forbid possession of nuclear weapons by those states which already have them.[5] Moreover, the treaty has some interesting non-parties, such as Algeria, Brazil, the People's Republic of China, France, Israel, and South Africa, all defendants in this action which, if they do not already possess nuclear weapons, could probably create them out of their own resources. It seems generally to have been assumed that non-parties are not bound by the general terms of the Treaty not to give or receive assistance in developing their own nuclear weapons capabilities, and some have certainly done so.

Under these circumstances, it is probably safe to conclude that treaty law does not reflect any sense that the mere possession of nuclear weapons is forbidden by general international law.

The second argument, based on a perceived analogy of nuclear weapons to bacteriological and toxin weapons, is more persuasive. The United States, the Soviet Union, and many other states are parties to a Convention dated 10 April 1972 providing for the destruction of existing stockpiles of such weapons along with the equipment and means of delivery associated with them.[6] Mere possession of those things is thus forbidden by treaty to parties known to have them. For our purposes, the question is whether this Convention codifies some more general rules forbidding the mere possession of weapons whose effects are too horrible to be tolerated by the consciences of political leaders no matter how they might be used. If so, a case might be made that an analogy exists between the effects of presently prohibited weapons and the effects of nuclear weapons as a class, thus allowing the same principles justifying their prohibition to be applied to the whole class.

This is, however, not the case. The consciences of political leaders over the centuries have been proved to be pretty insensitive. It is doubtful that the Convention reflects in any degree a conviction traceable to legal or moral principle. Instead, it seems much more likely that the Convention was the product of a calculation that possession of bacteriological and toxin weapons was a dubious military asset. Such weapons might be stolen with uncontrollable consequences in the possessing country itself. They might be released in that country by quick attack or guerrilla warfare against which there is no absolute defense. Those weapons have potentially uncontrollable effects even if used according to plan, and thus are not desirable battlefield weapons. Such practical considerations do not apply with equal force to nuclear weapons. Even if the effects of nuclear weapons are felt to be analogous to the effects of poisons, at this point the issue is possession, not use; conceding *arguendo* that analogous effects exist, the restrictions on possession of bacteriological and toxin weapons seem to stem from the undesirability of that possession, not the undesirability of their effects when used. The Convention reflects a calculation related to arms control expediency, not to moral principle. Thus, the analogy between bacteriological and toxin weapons on the one hand, and nuclear weapons on the other, from the point of view of analyzing the legality of mere possession, seems uncompelling.

As a matter of law, then, the mere possession of nuclear weapons of any type cannot be confidently held to be illegal in the absence of a treaty commitment forbidding that possession. Furthermore, the trends of the underlying general law do not seem to have moved far in the direction of forbidding that possession.[7]

C. Use of Nuclear Weapons

1. Direct Prohibition; *Per Se* Illegality

a. Treaty and State Practice

The use of nuclear weapons *per se* is not forbidden by any treaty,[8] although there are many United Nations General Assembly Resolutions, as well as some Red Cross and other international organization resolutions and documents on which at least a moral case can be built. The legal case is more subtle. To understand it, it is necessary first to mention that, although it is possible to argue that the negative precedent of the non-use of nuclear weapons since 1945 can be interpreted to have a pre-scriptive significance, the only affirmative state practice that seems arguably to have had legislative significance is the United States' dropping of two nuclear devices on Japan in 1945.

It is very difficult to see that catastrophe as a precedent either supporting the legality of using nuclear weapons or as evidence of illegality. In the final stages of the Pacific War the force of law forbidding excessive destruction or suffering was too weak to be tested by state practice; racial theories on both sides dehumanized the context and the enforcement pressures of reprisal and community reaction were absent. Moreover, the American decision to use the devices was apparently deliberately kept from normal official legal scrutiny by American political leaders both before and after the event.[9] Thus, rather than being consistent with an American view of what was permitted under the laws of war, the decision appears to have been a strictly political or military one taken in disregard of both morality and of law.

In one well-known case in 1963, a Japanese court held that the use of nuclear weapons by the United States against Japan in the Pacific War was a violation of the laws of war.[10] The court made that assertion in the course of upholding the validity in Japan of part of the 1951 Peace Treaty between the Japanese Government and the victorious allies, including the United States, waiving World War II war-injury claims by Japanese nationals for damages suffered through American violations of the laws and customs of war.[11] The court chastised the Government of Japan for entering into the treaty. Plaintiffs People of the Earth do not make much of that precedent here, and I think they are right. The opinion appears to test the use of the two nuclear devices against traditional legal restraints on the use of weaponry in war. However, by not distinguishing the use of nuclear weapons in principle from fire-bombing as practiced by the United States and its allies in Europe as well as in the Pacific phase of the war, or pillage and biological experiments practiced in China and elsewhere by Japan itself, the impression is left that the nuclear bombing by the United States was, and at the same time was not, distinguishable in kind from the other atrocities committed by both the United States and Japan during the war. Thus the court's conclusion seems self-contradictory.

Moreover, although the Japanese court castigated the political branches of the Japanese government for agreeing to waive some war crimes claims, the fact that the claims had been waived made moot all discussion of whether any particular acts by the United States were violations of the laws of war. Since the discussion had no legal relevance to the issues before the court, the court's logic has no more precedent value than the opinion of any publicist speaking in a vacuum. Nor did the court's decision reflect a balanced consideration of arguments for claims actually before the court; the substance of the claims was not argued. Indeed, even if the issue of the validity of Japanese claims for injury stemming from alleged war crimes had been before the court, the party seeking to show that particular acts were legitimate acts of war and not war crimes would have been the Government of Japan, not the United States. The United States was not a party to the case and presented no arguments to the court, nor could the structure of the legal order, logic, policy, or morality compel it to do so. In sum, the precedent value of the decision seems reduced to its inherent persuasiveness, and its logic seems less than compelling.

Many other arguments have been presented by various publicists and by Plaintiffs People of the Earth to support the proposition that any use of nuclear weapons is illegal. For example, the likely impact of nuclear fall-out or other incidental damage done to neutrals as a result of any use of nuclear weapons, has been alleged to make nuclear weapons *per se* illegal because *per se* indiscriminate.[12] But the actual practice of states illustrates the reverse. Wars frequently have an impact on the global commons and on neutrals and the incidental impact of war on neutrals has never been held to make the use of any weapon illegal as far as I have been able to ascertain. For example, belligerent sinkings of enemy vessels at sea have created oil slicks that damaged beaches during a war. Neither the injury to the global commons nor to the territory of any particular neutral has ever been the subject of formal complaint, much less arbitral or other awards, as far as I have been able to determine. A somewhat more compelling argument has been made regarding the inconsistency of national or allied use of nuclear weapons pre-empting the treaty-based peace-keeping role of the United Nations Security Council.[13] But again, the argument seems to be based on a reading of the United Nations Charter and other documents that is divorced from the interpretation given by the actual parties to those documents in their actual affairs. The argument loses touch with reality, and, therefore, cannot be persuasive as a matter of law, however persuasive as a matter of academic coherence or political goals.

Finally, the fact that no nuclear weapons have been used in war since 1945 seems not to be evidence that such use is considered to be forbidden by the law as much as evidence that it has seemed unwise as a matter of policy to use the weapons, whether or not that use would have been legally permissible. Certainly, nuclear weapons have been moved about in ways implying a willingness to use them from time to time, and the implications of those movements have been taken seriously by other states without legal arguments being raised.

b. Diplomatic Correspondence

In diplomatic correspondence, offers have been made by defendants the Soviet Union and the People's Republic of China for contract-like agreements to forbid "first use" of nuclear weapons. The intentions behind these offers can be variously interpreted, and the offers have been rejected by the United States and its North Atlantic allies. No country possessing nuclear weapons has raised an argument to the diplomatic level that first use is forbidden as a matter of law in the absence of a contract about it. Nor has any country offered to renounce use of nuclear weapons in reprisal against a nuclear attack against itself by others. These facts seem to indicate that whatever the views of political leaders on the politics or morality of first use, no legal or even humanitarian inhibition is felt regarding some use of nuclear weapons under some circumstances. Indeed, for deterrence to work, the other side must believe that the deterring power is willing as well as able to use the weapon in reaction to somebody else's first use.

Similarly, non-proliferation proposals, bans on testing and other arms control measures, seem to reflect an assumption that the development and deployment of nuclear weapons, as if for ultimate use, is entirely legal unless forbidden by treaty. Neither moral arguments against development and deployment, nor policy arguments regarding the impact of these activities on allies, antagonists, and constituents seem to have resulted in the international legal equivalent of legislation.

It is possible to suggest that all negotiations in an arms control context focus on the control of arms regardless of the legality of their use, that arms control specialists are as concerned with achieving a verifiable limit on an adversary's capability to fight with legal weapons as with illegal weapons, and that the distinctions between legal and illegal uses are thus irrelevant. From this point of view, the attitudes implied in the arms control agreements and diplomatic correspondence are evidence neither for nor against the legality of possible uses of nuclear weapons.

2. Indirect Prohibition: Analogy to Non-Nuclear Weapons

a. The General Rules

The most frequently stated arguments concerning the possible illegality of the use of nuclear weapons focus on their asserted cruelty and indiscriminacy. The basic rules are codified in the 1899/1907 Hague Regulations Respecting the Laws and Customs of War on Land:

Article 22: The right of belligerents to adopt means of injuring the enemy is not unlimited.

Article 23: In addition to the prohibitions provided by special Conventions, it is especially forbidden—

a. To employ poison or poisoned weapons; ...
e. To employ arms, projectiles, or material calculated to cause unnecessary suffering; ...
g. To destroy or seize the enemy's property, unless such destruction or seizure be imperatively demanded by the necessities of war.[14]

In addition, bombardment "by whatever means" of "towns, villages, dwellings, or buildings which are undefended is prohibited" (article 25) and in bombardments, all necessary steps must be taken to spare, as far as possible, buildings dedicated to religion, art, science, charitable purposes, historic monuments and the like (article 27). This last article has been further refined and expanded.[15] There are about 60 parties to either or both of the 1899 and 1907 Regulations, and the articles noted above are usually considered to codify general international law binding even on non-parties.

Despite its generality, article 22 is fundamental. The notion that the means of injuring an enemy is not unlimited—and the obvious implication that such limits as exist are not merely the technological limits on weapons or the policy interest of a belligerent, but relate to "the right" of belligerents—makes legal analysis necessary for the use of any type of weapon. It may seem to be wise policy to ignore the legal considerations involved in proposals to use nuclear weapons, but any state failing to incorporate those considerations in its actual policies would be placed in potential violation of its commitment to the 1899 and 1907 Hague Conventions or the general humanitarian law they reflect.

Article 23 can be read to forbid the use of nuclear weapons absolutely by those who regard their effects as analogous to the effects of poisonous weapons. The radiation effects of most nuclear weapons seem to bear some analogy to the effects of poisons, and the indiscriminacy with which these effects are distributed to noncombatant populations strengthens the analogy. On the other hand, the blast effects of nuclear weapons are more clearly analogous to artillery or aerial bombardment, simply (but not necessarily) bigger. Thus the argument is made that if "clean," or relatively fallout free "neutron" weapons are used, there is no significant analogy to "poisons," and even if "dirty" weapons are used, the "poisonous" effects of radiation are small compared to the blast effects, thus the analogy is misplaced. Lacking competence to analyze the blast and radiation effects of various nuclear weapons, or to compare them with the effects of various poisons, some of which, like tear gases, are argued to be permissible under technical interpretations of article 23 and other pertinent international agreements and practices accepted as law, it is difficult to come to any grand conclusions based on the analogy. I am satisfied that the use of at least some nuclear weapons used in some circumstances would be illegal on the basis of this analogy. I am not satisfied that all uses of nuclear weapons in all circumstances would be forbidden on the basis of the analogy to the prohibition on poison gases. It might also be pointed out that, as in the case of mere possession, the existing prohibitions on the use of bacteriological and toxin weapons, which also bear some analogy to poisons and to some categories and possible uses of nuclear weapons, appear to be based on arms control logic and not on any general international law forbidding their use, however immoral and politically self-defeating that use might be.

There is certainly an analogy between those nuclear weapons that have substantial poison-like effects and the "poison" whose use in war would be regarded by the world in general as forbidden by article 23(a) of the 1899 and 1907 Regulations regardless of technical distinctions that might convince some jurists otherwise. The existence of a legal argument appearing to justify something that seems analogous to poison in warfare will probably not be sufficient, either legally or politically, to avoid accusations and possible ultimate condemnation with the direst political and moral consequences. Nor, for advocates of the view that radiation is equivalent in law to poison, is there any problem with the usual legal position that those seeking to restrict the actions of states must show express or implied consent to that restriction by the state whose action is questioned.[16] That requirement has already been met by the ratification of the 1899 or 1907 Convention by nearly all of the defendants in this case and the established consensus that the cited articles of the Regulations appended to those Conventions now form part of general international law. The question is therefore not one of establishing the rule, but of interpreting the established rule.

Similar legal arguments can be made regarding the prohibition of destruction not "imperatively demanded by the necessities of war" and of arms apt to cause unnecessary suffering. If weapons more discriminating in their effects and less likely to produce suffering are available, then the military principles of economy of force reinforce the legal commitments of states. The use of nuclear weapons in a way that violates those universally recognized rules would be impermissible not only as a matter of law but as a matter of the honorable traditions of military policy as well.

The tendency to use excessive force in the later stages of

World War II, both in its European and Pacific phases, coupled with the normal military tactic that prefers a quick victory to a prolonged campaign, seem to play a role in some minds encouraging overwhelming overkill to force a rapid conclusion. But since there is no real inconsistency between military necessity and complete destruction of the enemy's military capabilities, the lines of legal distinction between permissible and impermissible destruction are sufficiently sharp. The argument that destruction of the civilian support structure, or the "will to resist," justifies such actions as the fire-bombing of Dresden seems defective in the calmer days of peace. Not only is it unclear that such destruction of indirect support and civilian facilities actually shortens the conflict in fact, but the logic of this approach carried just a bit further implies that genocide, the destruction of the enemy as a nation, is a legitimate military object. It is doubtful that any jurist familiar with the established laws of war or the Genocide Convention of 1948,[17] would make such an argument and it is unnecessary to address it seriously here. Moreover, as a political matter, to take such a position even in mere internal publicity would likely have the most demoralizing effects on allied constituencies and stiffen the will to resist of even the weakest of enemies. Finally, as a moral matter, to equate "victory" with the denial of all humanitarian values is to raise questions of value and even rationality that strike at the heart of the very notion of civilization. It must be rejected as a matter of law.

All of this does not totally eliminate the legal uses of nuclear weapons. No evidence has been presented to us that under the conventional or general international law of war all uses of nuclear weapons would be impermissible. The great destructive power of nuclear weapons as a class does not by itself make their use illegal any more than the increased power of steamships over wind-driven ships made armored gun platforms illegal. Attempts to limit the legal use of submarines as commerce destroyers after World War I, even when reduced to positive commitments, proved incapable of restricting that use in any significant way, and the conviction of Admiral Doenitz at Nuremberg on a charge of having ordered unrestricted submarine warfare in Europe does not establish a precedent in the light of the failure of any state to even propose that Admiral Nimitz of the United

States be tried on the same charge of having issued what he openly attested were nearly identical orders.[18]

b. Aerial Bombardment

Looking further at analogies to restrictions on the uses of conventional weapons in the law of war, we turn from a discussion of the general rules governing conventional warfare to rules relating to specific weapons. An analogy might be drawn between nuclear attack and aerial bombardment. Aerial bombardment can logically be considered a mere extension of artillery bombardment despite the difficulties of restricting bombs to legitimate targets. Blanket or indiscriminate bombing has been restrained in the past primarily by the fear of reprisal, but even this fear did not stop the devastation of non-military targets like Rotterdam by the Germans and Dresden by the allies during World War II, or Manila by Japan and large areas of Tokyo by the United States during the Pacific phase of that war.

An attempt to restrict aerial bombardment at the end of World War I resulted in the unratified draft Rules of Air Warfare of 1923. Article 22 forbids aerial bombardment "for the purpose of terrorizing the civilian population, or destroying or damaging private property not of military character, or of injuring non-combatants," and article 24 of which says that when military targets "are so situated, that they cannot be bombarded without the indiscriminate bombardment of the civilian population, the aircraft must abstain from bombardment."[19] These rules can, of course, be read as an invitation to a belligerent so to site its military installations within civilian residential or school areas as to make them seem immune from air attack. Such a reading would in practice be obviously unacceptable as a restriction on the enemy to destroy the military capacity of the belligerent so using its civilians as a legal shield. No belligerent is known to have accepted such a restriction on its own operations in any conflict.

Nonetheless, the principles adopted in these unratified rules are reflected in some treaties. Protocol III to the draft 1981 United Nations Convention on Prohibitions or Restriction on the Use of Certain Conventional Weapons Which May be Deemed to be Excessively Injurious or to Have Indiscriminate Effects forbids "in all circumstances" the air-delivery of incendiary devices against "any military objective located within a concentration of civilians."[20]

The 1923 rules were modified to some extent in the 1977 Protocol I to the 1949 Geneva Conventions,[21] which has not yet been ratified by the United States and other nuclear powers for stated reasons not related to this subject.[22] Articles 51 and 52 forbid attacks against all but military targets, including a prohibition on attacks "which may be expected to cause incidental loss of civilian life, injury to civilians, damage to civilian objects, or a combination thereof, which would be excessive in relation to the concrete military advantage anticipated."[23] Article 49 of that Protocol applies these rules specifically to attacks from the air. The 1981 Convention is restricted to non-nuclear weapons and, if conceived as an arms control agreement and not a codification of underlying general rules, seems irrelevant to this analysis. Indeed, the United States has been careful to try to structure its participation in the negotiations leading to both the 1977 Protocols and the 1981 Convention as strictly arms control exercises. In a declaration on signing Protocol I in 1977, the United States said that as far as it was concerned "the rules established by the protocol were not intended to have any effect on and do not regulate or prohibit the use of nuclear weapons."[24] The question did not arise overtly in the negotiation of the 1981 Convention because nuclear weapons were excluded from the purview of the rules being negotiated when the terms of reference for the negotiation were agreed. It is my view at this time, however, that such exclusions of particular classes of weapons from arms control arrangement cannot operate in law to exempt the uses of those excluded weapons from the normal rules of war, including those general rules, whether codified or not, that apply to all military activity. And if the negotiations and their products are regarded as not arms control bargains but reflections of specific customary or natural law rules applying to agreed classes of weapons, excepting nuclear weapons from the subject under negotiation cannot affect the applicability of those underlying rules to nuclear weapons. Indeed, the assertion that the rules do not regulate or prohibit the use of nuclear weapons does not amount to an assertion that the rules permit any use of nuclear weapons or release that use from the bond of legal restraint found outside the immediate occasion for the assertion. It might be supposed that any attempt to utter a declaration having that effect would have been so strongly resisted by the other parties to the conference that the very limited terms of the declaration itself can be taken as an indication that the consensus accepts the applicability of the general international law of war to the use of nuclear weapons.

D. CONCLUSIONS

The United States formally denies the applicability of the existing laws of war to nuclear weapons, not only in particular cases, but also in principle. The Soviet Union and perhaps other nuclear powers, possibly all the other defendants in this case, by their silence and military actions, including their stockpiling of nuclear weapons, take a similar position. The United States cannot be faulted for stating publicly a position that others adopt silently; indeed, the implication of hypocrisy lies more on the other defendants. Therefore, in the following comments aimed at an overt American position, it is the position of all the Defendants that is being discussed and the openness of the American position is considered worthy of praise and special commendation, whatever the legal merits of that position as such.

The United States position has long been that:

> The use of explosive 'atomic weapons', whether by air, sea or land forces, cannot as such be regarded as violative of international law in the absence of any customary rule of international law or international convention restricting their employment.[25]

This statement does not differentiate various possible uses of nuclear weapons and it can be read to imply, clearly incorrectly, that all uses of nuclear weapons can be regarded in customary international law as *prima facie* legal. It ignores the positive obligations of the United States under the general terms of the Hague Regulations of 1899 and 1907 which might indeed be considered to be "international convention[s] restricting their employment" because the Hague Regulations restrict the employment of all weapons of war. The United States position also seems to disregard the so-called "de Martens" clause of the Hague Conventions which specifically obliges parties, including the United States, to apply "the principles of the law of nations, as they result from the usages established among civilized peoples, from the laws of humanity and the dictates of the public conscience" in cases not specifically covered in the Regulations appended to the Conventions.[26] Thus, the implication of the formal American position, that there are no applicable restraints on the use of nuclear weapons in current conventional or customary international law, is simply false. Read more carefully, the American position might mean merely that its authors would accept whatever restraints conventional or customary law place on the use of nuclear weapons, but are not prepared to state publicly a position setting out what they conceive those restraints to be at this time.

Thus, two alternative conclusions can be drawn. One is that defendants regard nuclear weapons as legally merely a technological extension of conventional weaponry. Attempts to distinguish them from conventional weaponry can then be considered evidence of mere caution on the part of those states possessing nuclear weapons about their freedom to use them more than a real conviction that their use is legally permissible in circumstances where conventional weapons cannot legally be used. If this is a correct appreciation of the position taken by defendants, the legal limits on unnecessary destruction and suffering would apply to nuclear weapons as to all other classes of legal weaponry. That does not mean that all uses of nuclear weapons are illegal. Low fall-out, "clean" weapons in isolated battlefields, with a destructive capacity proportional to the military advantage anticipated from their use, would be entirely permissible. An obvious example of such a legal use might be in anti-submarine warfare, where casualties among non-combatants could be *de minimis* by the normal standards of armed conflict, the damage done by radioactive dust and other fallout almost negligible, and the military advantage potentially very great indeed, particularly if the target submarine is itself carrying nuclear weapons. Another use of nuclear weapons permissible in the absence of an arms control agreement could be to destroy an enemy's command communications or intelligence-gathering facilities in space. Indeed, deterrence of enemy attacks, even strictly conventional attacks, might be achieved by a legal capacity and demonstrated willingness to use lower-yield low-fallout weapons on military headquarters, rail yards and other clearly expansive military targets where the destruction would not be disproportionate to the military advantage anticipated by that use. On the other hand, under this rationale, so-called strategic bombing which resumes targeting where the excesses of World War II ended, with the equivalent of the legally doubtful fire-bombings of places whose military importance is dubious, would be illegal as well as politically foolish, militarily dishonorable, and morally beyond discussion.

The other possible legal conclusion is that nuclear weapons are a new class of weapon, legally distinguishable from conventional weapons, and that the rules that apply to their use have not yet been determined. Under this conclusion, in the absence of rules restricting that use, there are no legal restraints because the general rules do not apply to the sort of conflict that is not a "war" in the traditional sense; that the existence of nuclear weapons has changed the fundamental categories and created a new one, worse than "war," in which there are no legal restraints. If that is the view taken by states holding the capacity to use nuclear weapons, Armageddon is foreseeable. The notion that the more destructive the weapons the less restriction on its use seems so inconsistent with the very notion of civilization that it must be rejected. It appears to rest on the assumption that the natural state of mankind is a war of each against all, which seems the elevation of the oversimplified working model of a school of political theorists to the position of ideological basis for action in the real world. The law has always rejected that model, and I see nothing in the real world to indicate that the law has been wrong and that artificial model right. If public action is to be taken on the basis of that model, it must be without the concurrence of jurists.

I, therefore, conclude that neither the natural law nor the positive law forbids the development, deployment, or any other aspect of the possession of nuclear weapons; that both the natural law and the positive law contain major restrictions on the use of nuclear weapons; and that to the degree Defendants structure their military postures in disregard of the legal restraints on the use of nuclear weapons, they risk plunging the world into a political and moral chaos for which they will be answerable before a far higher tribunal than this. Recognizing that no amount of monetary damages can compensate for that injury, and that no threat of earthly punishment is available in the international legal order to deter states as such from such actions, and that the war crimes trials the international legal order permits for individuals' violations of the laws and customs of war are unlikely to deter even violations of this magnitude by the force-oriented people whom the political systems of the earth tend to put in positions of authority in the most militarily capable states part of the Federation of Earth, I conclude that an injunctive remedy is appropriate. Therefore, I would enjoin action by states and political leaders in planning for, and failing to plan feasible alternatives for, the use of nuclear weapons in all circumstances in which that use, including the threat of that use, is forbidden by public international law as set out herein.

Accordingly, with and to the full extent of the power vested in me as Judge of the Provisional District World Court of the Federation of Earth,

I DECLARE that the international humanitarian rules of war apply to nuclear weapons and their use in warfare, and that they severely restrict the use of such weapons in warfare;

I FURTHER DECLARE that the threat or use of nuclear weapons in ways forbidden by those rules in some cases cannot be compensable or properly the subject of reprisal under them, and that in all cases the threat or use of those weapons in ways forbidden by the international humanitarian rules of warfare is of sufficient interest to the general international community to justify that community in taking legal measures to prevent it;

I FURTHER DECLARE that under the view I take of the international legal order, "police action" and other coercive remedies analogous to the remedies the criminal law makes available to nearly all municipal legal orders, is not available in the absence of an international organization realistically capable of carrying out a law enforcement function; that the United Nations Security Council and other organs of the international legal order are not now able to discharge that function; that under the law of the Federation of Earth, an injunctive remedy is available analogous to the remedies many municipal legal orders give to civil claimants.

I, THEREFORE, GRANT to the Plaintiffs, The People of the Earth, an injunction forbidding the threat or use of nuclear weapons in any way violative of international law, including the international humanitarian rules of war.

Alfred P. Rubin
Judge, Provisional District, World Court

SEPARATE OPINION OF BURNS H. WESTON

Plaintiffs, The People of the Earth, claim, first, that the use of nuclear weapons is illegal under contemporary international law and, second, that the threat of use of nuclear weapons is illegal under contemporary international law. I respond to each of these claims hereinbelow.

A. The Use of Nuclear Weapons

1. I begin with the observation that, despite the tragedies of Hiroshima and Nagasaki,[1] the world community has yet to enact an explicit treaty or treaty provision generally prohibiting the development, manufacture, stockpiling, deployment, or actual use of nuclear weapons *per se*. It is true that a series of important treaties prohibit nuclear weapons in Antarctica, Latin America, outer space, and on the seabed beyond the limit of national territorial seas.[2] In addition, the 1963 Treaty Banning Nuclear Tests in the Atmosphere, in Outer Space and Under Water ("Partial Test Ban Treaty")[3] outlaws the testing of nuclear weapons in outer space, under water, and within the earth's atmosphere. And the recently ratified Treaty Between the United States of America and the Union of Soviet Socialist Republics on the Elimination of Their Intermediate-Range and Shorter-Range Missiles ("INF Treaty")[4] eliminates and prohibits an entire class of nuclear missiles and their delivery systems from the nuclear arsenals of the two superpowers. The fact remains, however, that despite these efforts to limit resort to nuclear weapons, there does not yet exist a *general* treaty ban on their use.

2. This fact is not lost on those who defend the legality of these weapons outside the foregoing treaty contexts. Consistent with the traditional State-centric theory of international legal obligation, which requires that prohibitions on international conduct be based on the express or implied consent of States, they rest their claim, in substantial part, on the proposition of the Permanent Court of International Justice in The Case of the S.S. Lotus (France v. Turkey),[5] to wit, that States are free to do whatever they are not strictly forbidden from doing. Indeed,

consistent with Cicero's oft-quoted but cynical maxim *inter arma silent leges* (in war the law is silent), some go so far as to contend that nuclear weapons have rendered the laws of war obsolete.

3.   But this does not end the matter. While the absence of an expicit general ban may mean that nuclear weapons are not illegal *per se*, it also is true that restraints on the conduct of war never have been limited to explicit treaty prohibitions alone. The law regulates implicitly as well as explicitly. Moreover, as stated by the International Military Tribunal at Nuremberg in September 1946, "[t]he law of war is to be found not only in treaties, but in the customs and practices of states which gradually obtained universal recognition, and from the general principles of justice applied by jurists and practiced by military courts."[6] It is, thus, to implicit as well as explicit treaty-based prescriptions and, in addition, to customary international law (involving the practice of States), to general principles of law (involving techniques of comparative law), and to all other pertinent "sources" of international legal authority and control (including, *inter alia*, judicial decisions, acts of international organizations, expressions of consensus, principles of equity, natural law, and the teachings of qualified publicists) that one turns before concluding that the use of nuclear weapons is in no way prohibited by the law of nations.

4.   A review of these "sources" or law-creating processes of international law compels, indeed, quite the opposite assessment, based on the following six core rules that one may derive from at least the conventional and customary laws of war:

first, that it is prohibited to use weapons or tactics that cause unnecessary and/or aggravated devastation and suffering;[7]

second, that it is prohibited to use weapons or tactics that cause indiscriminate harm as between combatants and noncombatant military and civilian personnel;[8]

third, that it is prohibited to effect reprisals that are disproportionate to their antecedent provocation or to legitimate military objectives, or that are disrespectful of persons, institutions, and resources otherwise protected by the laws of war;[9]

fourth, that it is prohibited to use weapons or tactics that cause widespread, long-term, and severe damage to the natural environment;[10]

fifth, that it is prohibited to use weapons or tactics that violate the neutral jurisdiction of non-participating States;[11] and

sixth, that it is prohibited to use asphyxiating, poisonous, or other gases, and all analogous liquids, materials, or devices, including bacteriological methods of warfare.[12]

"Scorched earth" and "saturation bombing" policies, incendiary and V-weapons, and the tendency generally to interpret the laws of war more in favor of the principle of military necessity than that of humanity naturally lead one to wonder about the vitality of these six core rules. However, despite these policies and practices, it still is correct to conclude that the six rules continue to count as law and that they are understood juridically to apply to nuclear as well as to so-called conventional weapons.

5. This conclusion is validated, first, in abundant expressions of legal expectation to the effect that nuclear weapons and warfare do not escape the judgment of these humanitarian rules. Indicative of a far-flung community consensus, they include *but are not limited to* the following:

5.1. The unanimous adoption by the United Nations General Assembly, on December 11, 1946, *after* the advent of the nuclear age, of Resolution 95(I),[13] recognizing the principles of international law formalized in the Nuremberg Charter,[14] including the definition of a "war crime" as embracing the "wanton destruction of cities, towns or villages, or devastation not justified by military necessity" and of a "crime against humanity" as involving "inhumane acts committed against any civilian population";

5.2. The negotiation and entry into force of the four 1949 Geneva Conventions on the humane conduct of war four years also *after* the advent of the nuclear age;[15]

5.3. United Nations General Assembly resolutions in 1961 and 1972 declaring the use of nuclear weapons to be "a direct violation of the United Nations Charter,"[16] "contrary to the rules of international law and to the laws of humanity,"[17] "a crime against mankind and civilization,"[18] and therefore a matter of "permanent prohibition";[19]

5.4. The dictum in the 1963 *Shimoda Case* (the only known judicial tribunal communication on the subject to date) holding that the bombings of Hiroshima and Nagasaki were contrary to international law in general and to the laws of war in particular;[20]

5.5. Resolutions of the International Committee of the Red Cross (which has come to play an important and respected quasi-official role in the implementation as well as the clarification and development of the humanitarian laws of war)[21] such as Resolution XXVIII of 1965 declaring: "The general principles of the law of war apply to nuclear and similar weapons";[22] and

5.6. The writings of publicists highly qualified in the field.[23]

6. Traditionalists will challenge reliance upon some or all of these expressions on the grounds that they are not "true sources" of law, or, in more functional terms, that their communicators lack the legal authority to prescribe. But this would be to suggest, erroneously, that only State actors have the legal competence to prescribe internationally respecting issues or values of major and universal significance, a viewpoint that contrasts sharply with the widespread understanding, certified in the famous Martens Clause of the 1907 Hague Convention IV and reaffirmed in the four 1949 Geneva Conventions and the two 1977 Geneva Protocols Additional, that the laws of war are in part a function of "the dictates of the public conscience."[24] Moreover, it is to beg the question of those sources that *are* acceptable by statist standards—for example, the 1925 Protocol for the Prohibition of the Use in War of Asphyxiating, Poisonous or Other Gases, and of Bacteriological Warfare,[25] which is so comprehensive in its prohibition that it has been authoritatively interpreted to interdict the use of nuclear weapons altogether.[26] Additionally, it is to overlook that there is little in the authoritative literature to indicate, either explicitly or implicitly, that nuclear weapons and warfare should *not* be subject to the humanitarian rules of armed conflict. As one highly qualified publicist has put it, emphatically:

> It would be scurrilous to argue that it is still *forbidden* to kill a *single* innocent enemy civilian with a *bayonet*, or wantonly to destroy a *single* building or enemy territory by *machine-gun* fire— but that it is *legitimate* to kill *millions* of enemy non-combatants and wantonly to destroy entire enemy cities, regions and perhaps

countries (including cities, areas or the entire surface of *neutral* States) by *nuclear* weapons.[27]

The world community has in no way consented to the abolition of the humanitarian rules of armed conflict in order to legitimize nuclear war.

7.   Also validating the conclusion that the humanitarian rules of armed conflict are understood juridically to apply to nuclear as well as to so-called conventional weapons is the fact that, for all that the nuclear-weapons States themselves may delay a general nuclear weapons ban, there nonetheless exists a community-wide *intention*—albeit clearly not yet a complementary *capacity*—to ensure the observance of the humanitarian rules of armed conflict relative to nuclear weapons and warfare. It is essential to observe this control intention because it is critical to the *opinion juris* that, jurists agree, causes normative propositions, formal as well as informal, to count as law (in this case the proposition that nuclear weapons and warfare are indeed subject to the humanitarian rules of armed conflict).

7.1. The intention is presently most conspicuous, certainly, in the communications that emanate from the nongovernmental sector among private individuals and groups who, though more or less powerless relative to national governments, nonetheless press—many of them—for the abolition of nuclear weapons and warfare altogether. The 1972 Stockholm Declaration of the U.N. Conference on the Human Environment (Principles 2 and 26),[28] the 1983 Pastoral Letter on War, Armaments and Peace of the National Conference of Catholic Bishops of the United States,[29] and the persistent labors of the quasi-official International Committee of the Red Cross (ICRC)[30] are prominently illustrative. Less prominent, perhaps, but no less significant, is the 1987 New York Anti-Nuclear Declaration of the Lawyers' Committee on Nuclear Policy (USA) and the Association of Soviet Lawyers (USSR).[31]

7.2. The control intention is evident, too, in the attitudes and behaviors of the non-nuclear weapons States. Although without the nuclear hardware to prove their restraint unequivocally, they may be seen to intend the regulation of nuclear weapons and warfare according to the humanitarian rules of armed conflict. For example, under the aegis and with the cooperation of the United Nations they have on numerous occasions expressed their resolve either to prohibit nuclear weapons *in toto* or to restrict their use severely according to the laws of war, and by increasingly large majorities.[32] Another example is seen in the so-called Delhi Declaration of January 28, 1985, issued by the Heads of State of Argentina, India, Mexico, Tanzania, Sweden, and Greece under the auspices of the "Five Continent Peace Initiative" of Parliamentarians Global Action.[33] Unmistakably, a large majority of the non-nuclear-weapons States are committed to the wholesale prohibition of nuclear weapons or, in the alternative, to their regulation according to the laws of war as at least most recently articulated.

7.3. Finally, there are the words and deeds of the nuclear weapons States themselves. Even while escalating nuclear capabilities and tensions to levels frightening even to sober observers, the nuclear powers appear to take for granted that nuclear weapons do not escape the scrutiny of the humanitarian rules of armed conflict. For example, a certain responsiveness to these rules—or in any event to the importance of not transgressing them—appears to have been at work, however perversely, in the bombings at Hiroshima and Nagasaki. Each were justified officially on grounds of military necessity.[34] Similarly, the responsiveness is present at least to some degree in the complete non-use of nuclear weapons in Korea, Vietnam, Afghanistan, and the Falkland/Malvinas Islands where, clearly, they could have been unleashed; likewise, to some degree, in the growing interest among United States and Soviet strategists in counterforce doctrine and capabilities for damage limitation.[35] But perhaps most significantly, the intention to make the humanitarian rules of war applicable to nuclear weapons and warfare is evident in the military manuals of the major powers, the purpose of which is, *inter alia*, to advise military personnel (particularly those in command positions) on how to comport themselves in time of war. The military manuals of the United States and the United Kingdom, for example, while denying the illegality of nuclear weapons *per se*, consistently instruct that nuclear weapons are to be judged according to the same standards that apply to other weapons in armed conflict.[36]

8.   In sum, despite an erosion over the years of legal inhibitions regarding the conduct as well as the initiation of war, there remains even in this thermonuclear age an inherited commitment to standards of humane conduct within which the reasonable belligerent can and must operate. Contrary to the repudiated *Kriegsraison* theory of the German war criminals, which argues that the "necessities of war" override and render inoperative the ordinary laws of war (*Kreigsmanier*), there remains the fundamental principle from which all the laws of war derive, namely, that the right of belligerents to adopt means and methods of warfare is *not* unlimited.[37]

9.   It is of course true that there exists a manifest ambiguity regarding the extent to which the humanitarian rules of armed conflict actually could be enforced in the event of a nuclear exchange. Yet it would be error to conclude that for this reason there is no international law placing nuclear weapons and warfare under their legal scrutiny. The fact that illegal acts sometimes go unpunished does not necessarily amount either to the acceptance of those acts or to the obliteration of the rule of law declaring them to be illegal. Indeed, if the contrary were true, there would be very little law to point to at any level of social organization.

10.   Furthermore, in view of the horrifying and potentially irreversible devastation of which nuclear weapons are capable, not to mention the very little time their delivery systems allow for rational thought, it is only sensible that all doubts about whether nuclear weapons are subject to the humanitarian rules of armed conflict, as a matter of law, should be answered unequivocally in the affirmative, as a matter of policy. Such a response is mandated, in any event, by a world public order that aspires to the shaping and sharing of values more by persuasion than by coercion; and it is in keeping, too, with the major trends of an evolving planetary civilization, embracing the persistent if uncertain quest for nuclear arms control and disarmament and the accelerating struggle for the realization of fundamental human rights, including the right to life and the emerging right to peace implicitly chartered in Article 28 of the Universal

Declaration of Human Rights.[38] Also, it is consistent with the spirit, if not always the letter, of the Nuremberg Charter,[39] the judgment rendered under it,[40] the Convention on the Prevention and Punishment of the Crime of Genocide,[41] and, not least, the Charter of the United Nations itself,[42] together with key General Assembly declarations and resolutions which are widely understood to be the authoritative interpretations of the Charter and, in particular, Article 2(4).[43]

11. I thus arrive at the conclusion that, while no treaty or treaty provision generally forbids nuclear weapons or warfare *per se* except in certain essentially isolated or limited circumstances, the conventional and customary laws of war (including the cardinal principle of proportionality that militates between the principles of military necessity and humanity) nevertheless proscribe, at a minimum, any first strike ("strategic," "theater-level," or "tactical") involving either "countervalue" or "counterforce" targeting, any second strike ("strategic," "theater-level," or "tactical") involving "countervalue" targeting, and probably most "strategic" and "theater-level" second strikes involving "counterforce" targeting—that is, almost every standard "strategic," "theater-level," and "tactical" option presently dominating at least Soviet and United States nuclear policy. A conscientious, contextual, and policy-oriented application of the humanitarian rules of armed conflict makes clear that whatever legal license is extended to the use of nuclear weapons it extends to no farther than: (a) very limited, mainly "battlefield" warfare utilizing low-yield, "clean," and accurate nuclear weapons for second use retaliatory purposes only; and (b) possibly—*but not unambiguously* until as yet undeveloped technological refinements are achieved—an extremely limited counterforce strike in "strategic" and "theater-level" settings also for second use retaliatory purposes only. Applying the humanitarian rules of armed conflict to different nuclear weapons options or uses, as international law clearly allows, tends to prove rather than disprove the illegality of these weapons generally.

B. The Threat of Use of Nuclear Weapons

12. The 1959 Antarctica Treaty,[44] the 1963 Partial Test Ban Treaty,[45] the 1967 Treaty of Tlatelolco,[46] the 1967 Outer

Space Treaty,[47] the 1971 Seabed Arms Control Treaty,[48] and the 1979 Agreement Governing the Activities of States on the Moon and Other Celestial Bodies ("Moon Treaty"),[49] explicitly prohibit nuclear weapons preparations short of actual combat use. Yet just as the world community has so far failed to enact an explicit treaty or treaty provision *generally* prohibiting the actual use of nuclear weapons *per se*, so also has it failed to enact an explicit treaty or treaty provision *generally* prohibiting the threat of use of nuclear weapons *per se*. Again, therefore, to determine the legal status of the threat of use of nuclear weapons, it is necessary to consult implicit as well as explicit treaty-based prescriptions and, in addition, customary international law, general principles of law, and all other "sources" of international legal authority and control that may be pertinent.

13. I begin by noting that if any given use of nuclear weapons is properly judged to be contrary to the humanitarian rules of armed conflict—*e.g.*, a first strike ("strategic," "theater-level," or "tactical") involving either "countervalue" or "counterforce" targeting, a second strike ("strategic," "theater-level," or "tactical") involving "countervalue" targeting, and probably most "strategic" and "theater-level" second strikes involving "counterforce" targeting—then logically any threat of such use should be considered contrary to the humanitarian rules of armed conflict as well. Such logic is encouraged, in any event, by general principles of law derived from domestic legal systems that guard against "inchoate crimes" (involving, for example, threats and conspiracies to commit unlawful acts) and by basic notions of moral philosophy that insist upon at least the immorality, if not always the illegality, of threats or conspiracies to commit immoral and unlawful acts.

14. I note also Article 2(4) of the Charter of the United Nations,[50] which prohibits, *inter alia*, "the threat ... of force against the territorial integrity or political independence of any state, or in any other manner inconsistent with the Purposes of the United Nations." Inasmuch as any of the standard strategic and theater-level nuclear warfaring options mentioned above would, if exercised, impact severely—most likely irretrievably— upon the territorial integrity *and* political independence of a target State, not to mention the purposes of the United Nations, one may reasonably conclude that, in general, a threat of such

nuclear force would constitute a violation of Article 2(4). It would violate also the authoritative commentaries upon Article 2(4), to wit, the U.N. General Assembly's 1974 Resolution on the Definition of Aggression,[51] its 1970 Declaration on Principles and of International Law Concerning Friendly Relations and Co-operation Among States in Accordance with the Charter of the United Nations,[52] and its Declaration on the Inadmissibility of Intervention in the Domestic Affairs of States and the Protection of their Independence and Sovereignty,[53] which either explicitly or implicitly likewise prohibit the threat of the use of force.

15.   Now if the lawfulness or unlawfulness of any particular activity is to be based only on its congruity with some authoritative principle or text, it would be unnecessary to proceed any further. However, the complexities that attend the phenomenology of threat and the interrelation of that phenomenology with the public order sanctioning goals of prevention and deterrence recommend otherwise, particularly as the goals of prevention and deterrence resound in Article 51 of the U.N. Charter,[54] safeguarding "the inherent right of individual or collective self-defense" in case of an "armed attack." A clearly articulated official communique credibly indicating a nuclear attack if certain concrete demands are not met likely falls within the zone of prohibition. So, too, would an ostentatious brandishing of nuclear arms, such as a menacing "demonstration burst," designed to frighten an adversary into some manner of submission. Indeed, it is reasonable to presume as unlawful even the commonplace advance preparation of nuclear missiles for immediate launch. But, assuming "threat" is to be defined as much by the perceptions of the receiver as by the intentions of the maker of the threat, is the entire remaining continuum (or remaining properties) of nuclear threat—ranging from legislative appropriation, to research and development, to manufacture, to stockpiling, to deployment separating warheads from delivery systems—likewise susceptible to suppositions of illegality? It is not enough simply to cite Article 6(a) of the Nuremberg Charter,[55] which defines "crime against peace" to mean the "planning, preparation, initiation or waging of war of aggression, or a war in violation of international treaties, agreements or assurances, or participation in a common plan or conspiracy for the accomplishment of any of the foregoing," and notwithstanding that

this rule like other rules of the law of war applies to nuclear weapons and warfare as much as it does to conventional weapons and warfare? International law does not prohibit all forms of threat any more than it prohibits all forms of coercion, and thus Article 6(a) and other such formulations must be treated more as rebuttable presumptions than as definitive conclusions, until at least the function or purpose of the nuclear threat is known. However much the cause of world peace and justice might be enhanced by banning all threats of nuclear force, it is essential in the existing decentralized global order at least to consider such questions as whether or not the threat of nuclear force is meant to serve a policing function to ensure compliance with, say, a fundamental international human rights norm such as the prohibition of genocide; whether or not it is expected to accelerate the peaceful—*i.e.*, nonforcible—resolution of a potentially catastrophic conflict or dispute; or whether or not it is intended to play the role of "ritualized substitute" for aggressive violence, serving to dissuade international actors from resorting to violence (as typically the strategy of nuclear deterrence is justified). Additionally, the intensity of the threat and the severity of the consequences potentially flowing from it must be seen as conditioning factors.

16. These complexities and subtleties are not adequately addressed by the Plaintiffs. Indeed, they scarcely are addressed in the legal literature.[56] Accordingly, I am able to respond to Plaintiffs' request for declaratory judgment on the legality of the threat of use of nuclear weapons only in the most general, provisional terms. Summarizing my discussion in Paragraphs 12-15, above, I rule that international law establishes a rebuttable presumption against the legality of the threat of use of nuclear weapons at least insofar as such threat represents an imminent possibility of the illegal use of nuclear weapons as hereinabove identified.

* * *

17. It would be of course naive to expect that the law alone can rid the world of nuclear weapons and the threat or actuality of nuclear warfare. Nevertheless, it is essential to the evolution of a peaceful and just global polity that the strategic planners

and apologists among the nuclear weapons States—especially the defense policy-makers, the military operators, the laboratories of military research and development, the arms controllers, the politicians, even the jurists—come to see the essential incompatibility of nuclear weapons and warfare with the core precepts of international law. More and more have they got to change their modes of thinking. More and more must they be made to understand that the bell tolls for us all.

18. Accordingly, with and to the full extent of the power vested in me as Judge of the Provisional District World Court of the Federation of Earth,

I DECLARE that the international humanitarian rules of armed conflict are not obsolete, that they apply to nuclear weapons and warfare, and that they severely restrict the use of such weapons and warfare in almost all instances, especially in relation to the standard "strategic" and "theater-level" options that dominate Soviet and United States nuclear policy;

I FURTHER DECLARE that the threat of use of nuclear weapons is presumptively impermissible under contemporary international law when such a threat is direct and acutely menacing, but that, until a thorough appraisal of the phenomenology of nuclear threat indicates otherwise, essentially cautious, long-term preparations for preventing or deterring nuclear war are not impermissible under contemporary international law; and

I THEREFORE GRANT to the Plaintiffs, The People of the Earth, such injunctive relief as they have requested that is consistence with these findings.

DATED: July 1, 1988

Burns H. Weston
Judge, Provisional District, World Court

II.

Excerpts from the Ruling of the London Nuclear Warfare Tribunal

Introduction

The Relevance of International Law

At the outset, we are aware of public skepticism. Many citizens and public officials continue to query whether international law is *really* law in the absence of police mechanisms for enforcement and the absence of procedures for impartial interpretation. Our response here is that international law provides the underpinning for many varieties of transnational life that work so well we take it for granted. An effective legal order does not necessarily depend on central institutions for decision and enforcement. Law can be effective if the parties seek to make it so out of reasons of convenience, mutual benefit, a sense of right and respect, or even because they find value in a reputation of law-abidingness. These factors all operate to some extent in international life, varying from one substantive area to another, and from one kind of leadership to another.

Of course, all law is violated at times. Indeed, enforcement would be superfluous were compliance perfect. The special problem of international life arises because some violations are so totally disruptive and unacceptable in their effects. It is important to be clear that preventing a particular kind of violation is a different challenge to a legal order than a denial of its existence altogether.

There is no doubt that considerations of reciprocity which ensure a high degree of effectiveness for international law (e.g. upholding the immunity of foreign diplomats to reinforce the immunity of our own) are least operative in the context of war and peace where fundamental security, even survival, is at stake. Again, the wider context is important to appreciate. All law tends to bend and break in conditions of crisis, as is evident during periods of civil strife or economic privation.

Nevertheless, even governments have acknowledged over the centuries the great importance of bringing law to bear on decisions associated with *recourse to* and the *conduct of* war. From Grotius onward there has been a consensus to the effect that unrestrained warfare was a regression to barbarism, unacceptable as such. Especially in the last century or so there has been a dual series of developments: first of all, the technological innovations in warfare, culminating in the development and use of atomic bombs; secondly, an intensifying insistence on restricting the discretion of governments to wage war "legally".

There is no doubt that the possession of nuclear weapons underscores the tension between those political developments that give the modern state unconditional power over human destiny and those normative reactions by civil society that seek to impose limits upon what governments can do, even beneath the banners of military necessity and national security. There is no doubt also that since 1945 the statists have prevailed in relation to warfare and weaponry of mass destruction. There have been many wars and relatively little success in resolving conflict by recourse to the procedures made available by international law and embodied in the United Nations.

The leading nuclear weapons states have claimed that their possession of such weaponry has probably prevented World War III, and that the only reliable method to sustain "peace" is to threaten the annihilation of a rival society in retaliation. This system of mutual threat is generally called deterrence, and its logic and probable effects are not reconcilable with most understandings of law and morality. This Tribunal proceeded on the assumption that such a departure from normative restraint is dangerous and unacceptable, and that it does entail a relapse into barbarism on the grandest imaginable scale.

This Tribunal takes cognizance of both sides of this modern

dilemma. Firstly, the urgent need to replace deterrence with a system of international security responsive to law and morality. Secondly, the realization that governments and their institutional creations, including the United Nations, are not sufficiently motivated or empowered to satisfy this most fundamental of international needs. In these regards, this Tribunal is filling a normative vacuum. It intends to mobilize public opinion throughout the world around the necessity to bring available law to bear on the nuclear-weapons policies of governments.

It is, at the same time, important to realize that this Tribunal has not invented the legal framework it relies upon. This framework has evolved over the years by governmental action responding to felt necessities and to the aspirations of the peoples of the world. We shall endeavor to demonstrate clearly that the international law interpreted and applied by this Tribunal is of a status that should be applied by governments themselves.

In this respect, the Tribunal was convened to fill a constitutional gap in the international political system of the present. Its existence is an enactment of the call for individual responsibility that is itself a signal achievement of modern international law and has been heralded as such by the main nuclear weapons states.

It is a startling irony that, aside from China, the other states that now acknowledge possession of nuclear weapons constituted the four prosecuting states at Nuremberg after World War II. In particular the two superpowers, the United States and the Soviet Union, were most insistent that German leaders at all levels of society be held criminally liable for their refusal to uphold international law in the context of war and peace.

The victorious governments were emphatic that their proceedings against the defeated governments of Germany and Japan would provide a framework for all political activities in international life. After the judgments had been given, a consensus among the victorious governments supported the effort to formulate the Nuremberg Principles as universally binding rules of international law. These Principles impose on governments and officials an unconditional duty to uphold international law regardless of state policy. This Tribunal believes that this duty serves the interests of all peoples, and that even the interest of one's own country is best upheld by assuring that its policies abroad conform to the rules of international law. It is then a matter of patriotic duty to insist on the application of the Nuremberg Principles, most especially in relation to nuclear weaponry, where to await an entire breakdown of order before establishing the full evidence of a violative pattern of conduct would be too late.

It is true that, at the time of the Nuremberg Judgment, and ever since, critics have dismissed the whole enterprise as "victors' justice." There was a somber truth to this contention. As the Indian member of the Tokyo Tribunal, Justice Pal, pointed out, it was unacceptably hypocritical to accuse Japanese war leaders of crimes but exempt from scrutiny the Western indiscriminate bombing of Japanese cities climaxing in the atomic attacks on Hiroshima and Nagasaki. This Tribunal acknowledges the imperfections in the legal precedents, but seeks to build upon them to complete their promise.

It can also be alleged that the nuclear weapons states have not clearly accepted the view that these weapons are illegal. This Tribunal carefully considered this allegation, but feels convinced by the evidence that international law exists with sufficient clarity to assess the policies of governments with respect to nuclear weapons. This Tribunal agrees that a comprehensive treaty of prohibition would be a contribution to the avoidance of nuclear war, but that even without such a document, existing treaties and customary rules of international law are clear on these matters.

Substantive Foundations

This Tribunal is not inventing law. It has relied upon the best available experts on the international law of war to ascertain the character of rules applicable to nuclear weapons policy. These experts were cross-examined by trained legal counsel and by the members of the Tribunal itself. To introduce the Judgment, a brief survey is provided of the sources of international law applicable here.

1.   Just War Doctrine

Originating in theological discourse during the Middle Ages, the so-called Just War Doctrine was incorporated into positive international law. Drawing on still more ancient practices of political communities, the Just War Doctrine called upon participants in war to carry on combat with due respect for moral principles, including an overriding obligation to confine military attack to military targets , thereby avoiding any direct injury to civilians.

The application of the principles of the Just War Doctrine was left to each sovereign ruler, and amounted to an appeal to conscience. There was no higher authority aside from the questionable claim by the Roman Church which lost whatever overall validity it might have once possessed due to the fragmenting of Christendom during the Reformation of the sixteenth century. In a sense, the Just War Doctrine was an instance of religious morality being converted into an applied ethics for international relations. It was borrowed and incorporated into international law at the inception of the state system.

2.   Customary Norms of International Law

The lack of specificity in the Just War Doctrine was a shortcoming, as was the absence of any ritual of assent by which a sovereign authority acknowledged its duty to be bound in definite ways. International jurists collected the body of practices that governments accepted as binding upon themselves, and set forth these rules and principles beneath the label of customary international law. These rules and principles helped shape the direction of treaty law, and, as well, provided legally accepted yardsticks for measuring claims about the status of new weapons and tactics. Such rules and principles provide a normative background against which to evaluate the controversy about the lawfulness of nuclear weapons and about various doctrines governing their use.

Principle of Discrimination. To be lawful, weapons and tactics must discriminate clearly between military and non-military targets, and be confined in their application to military targets. Indiscriminate warfare is *per se* illegal, although indirect damage to civilians and civilian targets is not necessarily so.

Principle of Proportionality. To be lawful, weapons and tactics must be proportional to their military objective. Disproportionate weaponry and tactics are excessive, and as such, illegal.

Principle of Lawfulness. To be lawful, weapons and tactics must not violate any treaty rule of international law binding as between the parties.

Principle of Necessity. To be lawful, weapons and tactics involving the use of force must be reasonably necessary to the attainment of their military objective. No superfluous or excessive application of force is lawful, even if the damage done is confined to the environment.

Principle of Humanity. To be lawful, no weapon or tactic can be relied upon that causes unnecessary suffering to its victims, whether by way of prolonged or painful death, or in a form that is calculated to cause severe terror or fright. For this reason, weapons and tactics that spread poison, disease, or do genetic damage are generally illegal *per se*, as being weapons with effects not confined in the place and time of damage to the battlefield. Such a prohibition, under contemporary circumstances, extends to ecological disruption in any form.

Principle of Neutrality. To be lawful, no weapon or tactic can be relied upon that seems likely to do harm to human beings, property, or the natural environment in neutral countries. A country is neutral if its government declares itself to be so and if it pursues a policy of impartiality in relation to armed conflict, including the avoidance of any kind of alliance relationship.

3.   Treaty Rules and Principles

Often it is assumed, wrongly, that international agreements in treaty form are the only valid source of international legal obligations. In some respects, written agreements, duly ratified, are preferable sources of guidance as to the requirements of international law. Written formulations can be more explicit and elaborate with respect to a given pattern of conduct. Furthermore, as far as governments are concerned, there is a tendency to accord greater respect to those legal obligations to which consent in explicit and constitutional form has been given, especially if the negotiation and ratification processes are recent, most particularly within the life span of the governmental leadership currently in power.

There are also limitations to the view that treaty rules are the only genuine source of international law, or that these formulations of law are necessarily the best source. Some general norms have not been reduced to treaty form. In other instances, some states are not bound by treaties, having withheld their consent. In still other instances, the content of treaty rules is vague or subject to contradictory formulations, especially so in relation to the early efforts to codify war and peace, quite dramatically superseded by modern methods and styles of warfare, as well as by new military technologies and weapons systems. This Tribunal has applied international law by taking full account of both customary and treaty rules of international law.

There is an obvious problem of application with respect to nuclear weapons. The nuclear weapons states have so far refrained from entering into any serious negotiations towards a treaty, or even a declaration, acknowledging the unlawfulness of threats or uses of nuclear weapons. Such a deficiency is obviously not an oversight. Hence, to derive applicable rules of international law that add up to an unconditional prohibition of the use of this weaponry is bound to collide with the official security policies of major states, and to challenge the legitimacy of weapons capabilities and bureaucracies that command control over vast allocations of resources.

There are, however, certain broad efforts to reduce to treaty form agreed standards of behavior that seem crucial here, especially because their generality suggests a relevance to any assessment of the lawful status of nuclear weapons and tactics. The important general treaties in this area were formulated at the Hague in 1899 and 1907 in a series of comprehensive conventions that summarized the pre-World War I levels of agreement as they existed between the governments playing a leading role in international life. The goal was not to eliminate war, but to regulate its conduct in accordance with the customary principles briefly set forth in the preceding paragraph. Especially important was the broad imperative embodied as a common article in the various Hague Conventions of 1899. Article 22 in the Annex to the Hague Convention IV (Regulations Respecting the Laws and Customs of War on Land) states: "The right of belligerents to adopt means of injuring the enemy is not unlimited." The apocalyptic implications of a major reliance on nuclear weapons gives this provision an obvious orienting relevance.

Also critical was the celebrated Martens Clause (named after the Belgian jurist Feodor de Martens) inserted in the 1907 Hague Conventions:

> Until a more complete code of laws of war has been issued, the high contracting Parties deem it expedient to declare that, in cases not included in the Regulations adopted by them, the inhabitants and belligerents remain under the protection and the rule of the principles of the law of nations, as they result from the usages established among civilized people, from the laws of humanity, and the dictates of the public conscience.

This resolve in international treaty law to base permissible action expressly on normative traditions and upon conscience is a significant basis of encouragement for the inquiry of this Tribunal. The Martens Clause definitely refutes the ultra-statist view that everything is permissible if it has not been expressly renounced by a formal manifestation of governmental authority.

International treaty law has successfully achieved a very widely endorsed prohibition of poison as a weapon and tactic of war. To date the most important treaty instrument, adopted in response to the menace of poison gas revealed in the trenches of World War I, is the 1925 Geneva Protocol for the Prohibition of the Use in War of Asphyxiating, Poisonous and other Gases, and of Biological Methods of Warfare. At present a variety of negotiations and proposals seek to extend in more detailed form this prohibition on toxic weaponry. Unlike in the case of biological weapons, the current treaty law prohibits threat and use, but not development and possession. Hence, a deterrent approach to chemical weapons is not *per se* prohibited under contemporary international law.

Another significant line of effort in treaty law concerns the discretion to initiate war via acts of aggression. In the 1928 Pact of Paris (the Kellogg-Briand Pact), war is outlawed as an instrument of national policy, and legitimate force confined to circumstances of self-defense. This treaty norm provided a major basis for the war crimes prosecution at Nuremberg and Tokyo after World War II, giving rise to the category of offense known as "Crimes Against Peace." The United Nations Charter, a multilateral treaty, carries forward in articles 1(4), 33, and 51 the basic notion that there is no legal pretext for recourse to force in international relations except in self-defense against a prior attack. There is some controversy among international law specialists as to whether patterns of state practice have so consistently ignored this constraining legal framework as to suspend, or to draw into question, its continuing validity. At stake in the nuclear weapons setting is the critical issue as to whether the design and development of first-strike weaponry and supporting doctrine amounts to a *per se* act of aggression, as well as rendering officials liable for crimes against the peace. At Nuremberg it was definitely decided that planning for aggressive war is itself a crime even if the aggressive policy is never consummated. Does this prohibition pertain to those allegations that certain classes of nuclear weapons systems have first-strike properties and roles?

Another major treaty instrument was the Genocide Convention of 1948 that established the criminality of any course of deliberate state policy that intends to destroy, in whole or in part, national, ethnic, religious, or racial groups. Nuclear weapons are aptly described as weapons of mass destruction, and their use in any sustained manner seems genocidal in impact, as well as ecocidal. Indeed, the grim magnitude of such destruction suggests that beyond genocide lies the result of omnicide. Given the inability to apprehend after the event, this Tribunal seeks to examine whether the genocidal propensities of nuclear weapons, and doctrines governing their use, do not constitute sufficient ground to find governments and their leaders guilty of intentional violations of the Genocide Convention.

Ever since the nineteenth century there has been an effort complementary to that of the Law of the Hague dealing with weapons and tactics to codify international humanitarian law applicable during wartime, sometimes known as the Law of Geneva, because so many of the main treaty instruments were negotiated and signed at Geneva. The main elements of the Law of Geneva are the four Geneva Conventions of 1949—for the protection of land forces, of sea forces, of prisoners of war, and of civilians. The attempt of these agreements is to give concrete application to the Principle of Humanity, by imposing obligations on belligerent states to respect the sanctity of such things as hospitals, cultural monuments, etc., and to avoid any military action against the sick and wounded, or against those of the enemy who have laid down their arms and become prisoners of war.

These treaty rules suggest levels of respect for the limits of warfare that seem utterly inconsistent with any use of nuclear weapons. Again an issue for this Tribunal is whether this body of law can be superseded by contrary patterns of state practice. Efforts to extend this humanitarian approach to the explicit circumstances of nuclear weaponry have not been successful as yet. Both the United States and Britain made it clear that its participation in the negotiation of the Geneva Protocols I and II in 1977, to modernize the 1949 Conventions, was taking place on the assumption that nuclear weapons were not to be considered subject to the treaty norms, even in relation to article 35 which explicitly deals with new weapons and methods of warfare. Is such an exclusion effective? This question is important for this Tribunal to address in its Judgment.

A final source of treaty guidance for this Tribunal arises from the legal duty imposed on the governments of nuclear states by such arms control agreements as the Limited Test Ban Treaty of 1963 and the Non-Proliferation Treaty of 1968, to negotiate in good faith an end to the nuclear arms race and to establish by stages or any reasonable process, secure arrangements for general and complete disarmament. This Tribunal needs to determine whether the failure to accept proposals for a comprehensive test ban and the continued preparation for nuclear warfare, including the development of new weapons systems with first-strike propensities, amount to violations of international treaty obligations.

4.   Supplementary Norms with Legal Force

The United Nations has itself contributed in a variety of respects to the development of international law. General Assembly resolutions have been claimed to have a limited legislative effect under certain conditions of their passage. The U.N. General Assembly has manifested its concern about the lawful status of nuclear weapons in a long series of widely endorsed resolutions going back to General Assembly Resolution 1603 (XVI), which clearly supported the view that threats or uses of nuclear weapons were violations of the U.N. Charter and constituted Crimes against Humanity. The United States and its NATO allies voted against this and other subsequent resolutions on this subject matter. Does its oposition undermine or erode the legal force of General Assembly efforts in this area?

A closely related concern involves the status of initiating use of nuclear weapons. Both the Soviet Union and China made in 1981 a unilateral and unconditional commitment never to use nuclear weapons first. The Western nuclear powers have not acceded in any formal way to this no-first-use position. What status the no-first-use position has in contemporary international law is an important issue for this Tribunal to examine.

Natural law criteria of state behavior are also applicable through a continued reliance on the Marten's Clause and its invocation of the "laws of humanity" and "the dictates of public conscience." Such a moral outreach *within international law* makes it important and entirely appropriate to consider for legal relevance the great variety of statements by religious bodies describing their urgent concern and supporting reasoning about the irreconcilability of current doctrines pertaining to the use of nuclear weapons and the dictates of public conscience. Such an assessment is reinforced by a growing number of independent experts lending their professional judgment to the view that current policies of nuclear weapons states violate international law in flagrant and serious ways and to varying degrees. Such materials by religious bodies or international jurists are not law as such, but evidence as to the content of law, especially given the legal duty by governments to respect the dictates of public conscience in their war-making activities.

Method of Inquiry

This Tribunal is an informal body without any official mandate. At the same time, it is totally independent and no one connected with its activities received any kind of compensation for their efforts. The Judges were selected by the Convenors and listened to the evidence as presented by expert witnesses and in documentary submission. It sought arguments *pro* and *contra* the main issues in as effective form as was available. On its own the Tribunal examined additional materials as relevant for the discharge of its functions.

The Judgment will discuss the probable effects of nuclear weapons if they are ever used again, and rely on this analysis to infer the probable intentions of responsible civilian and military officials. As in domestic law, a person is held responsible for the probable effects of his actions whether or not a specific result is willed. Such accountability is even more appropriately imposed on a collective entity such as a government. This process of ascertaining and applying legal standards is especially appropriate where the burden of social policy is *preventive* rather than *reactive*. The circumstances posed by the nuclear arms race and the doctrine of deterrence make such a preventive emphasis *in the law* of decisive and overwhelming importance. After analyzing the evidence as carefully as possible the Tribunal will present its conclusions, followed by a set of policy recommendations. In a broad sense, this Tribunal is carrying on in the spirit of Nuremberg which above all else imposes on individual citizens the duty to safeguard international peace and security by making sure that governments uphold their obligations under international law. It is also trying to clarify "the dictates of public conscience" on the matter of legal duty pertaining to nuclear weaponry, and thereby responding to the call of the Martens Clause. And finally, it joins with such kindred entities as the Permanent People's Tribunal to support the legitimacy and importance of societal initiatives to encourage adherence to international law in the war/peace area, and claims for itself authority to declare the character of legal obligations in relation to nuclear weapons that is owed by governments, officials, military officers, scientists and engineers, as well as by citizens occupying various roles in society.

Overview of Tribunal Scope

The primary enquiry of the Tribunal was *"An Examination of the Legality of Nuclear Weapons."* As an acceptable standard of lawfulness they have taken the six principles identified above, namely:

1.   Principle of Discrimination
2.   Principle of Proportionality
3.   Principle of Lawfulness
4.   Principle of Necessity
5.   Principle of Humanity
6.   Principle of Neutrality

As part of that examination the Tribunal posed and endeavored to answer two fundamental questions:

1.   Does international law forbid the use of nuclear weapons, and

2.   Does international law forbid the possession of nuclear weapons?

The Tribunal received evidence under four main headings:
1.   The medical and environmental effects of nuclear attack
2.   Current weaponry and strategy
3.   The moral implications
4.   The legal implications

The task of the Tribunal was to make findings of fact on the evidence and in particular of the behavior and intentions of the nuclear weapon states and of the likely effects of that behavior and those intentions. Those findings have been compared with the standards set by the six principles.

Chapter 1

Relevant International Law

This section summarizes the evidence from witnesses about International Law which is relevant to the possession and use of nuclear weapons.

Lawfulness of Nuclear Weapons—-Position of Nuclear States

Professor Meyrowitz stated the U.S. position as to the legal status of nuclear weapons under international law thus: "The official U.S. position is that there is no expressed prohibition in international law or formal treaty or clause in a convention that prohibits the use of nuclear weapons."

The U.S.S.R.'s position was stated by Dr. Vlasikhin as follows: "Although the existing instruments, conventions, and Geneva Protocols prohibit weapons of mass destruction, and obviously nuclear arms fall under this category, still there is no specific prohibition of nuclear arms."

The British position was stated in correspondence from the British Foreign Office, whilst declining the Tribunal's invitation to give evidence: "The Government's considered and firm view is that there is no aspect of current defense policy which is inconsistent with the United Kingdom's obligations under international law, including the laws of war. Britain and NATO possess nuclear weapons only to deter aggression. NATO leaders gave a solemn undertaking in Bonn in 1982, repeated in Brussels in December 1983, that no NATO weapon, be it conventional or nuclear, would ever be used except in response to aggression. NATO possesses nuclear weapons not to fight war but to prevent one ever occurring."

Sources of International Law

According to the evidence before the Tribunal, several sources of international law were identified by various witnesses and

deponents to include (this is not intended as an exhaustive list):
* the United Nations Charter (to which all nuclear weapons states are a party)
* other treaties and similar written documents
* customary international law
* highly qualified publicists of international law
* general principles of law recognized by civilized nations
* public conscience
* laws of humanity

Relevant Treaties, Declarations, and Conventions

This section briefly surveys several of the key treaties which affect the international law of war.

1.   The St. Petersburg Declaration of 1868

The St. Petersburg Declaration of 1868 is regarded as the first international legal instrument prohibiting weaponry. It was made following a conference convened by Czar Alexander II to deal with the recently invented explosive bullets. The preamble to the Declaration sets out the following two principles:

a)   The only legitimate object which states should endeavor to accomplish is to weaken the military forces of the enemy;

b)   That for this purpose it is sufficient to disable the greatest possible number of men; that this object would be exceeded by the employment of arms which uselessly aggravate the sufferings of disabled men or render their deaths inevitable; that the employment of such arms would therefore be contrary to humanity.

2.   The Hague Conventions of 1907

The preamble to the fourth Hague Convention of 1907 has become known as the Martens Clause, after its author. The clause has been duplicated and adopted in nearly all the major 20th century treaties of the laws of war. The nuclear weapons states consider themselves bound by the clause. It states as follows: "Until a more complete code of the laws of war has been issued, the high contracting Parties deem it expedient to declare that, in cases not included in the Regulations adopted by them, the inhabitants and belligerents remain under the protection and the rule of the principles of the laws of nations, as they result from the usages established among civilized people, from the laws of humanity, and the dictates of the public conscience."

The main body of the Hague conventions reaffirmed and expanded what is stated in the St. Petersburg Declaration in 1868:

- that the right of a belligerent to adopt means to injure the enemy is not unlimited.

It expanded and forbade:

- the employment of poison or poisoned weapons;
- the killing or wounding treacherously of individuals belonging to the hostile state or army;
- the employment of arms, projectiles, or material calculated to cause unnecessary suffering;

It also went further by prohibiting:

- the destruction or seizure of enemy property unless such destruction was unnecessary ; and
- attacks on undefended villages and towns.

The Hague Conventions reaffirmed that religious, artistic, scientific, or charitable buildings should be spared as much as possible during a siege, as well as historical monuments and places where the sick and wounded are cared for.

By Hague Convention V, the territory of neutral powers was made inviolable (Article 1, Convention (V) Respecting the Rights and Duties of Neutral Powers and Persons in Case of War on Land).

3.   Geneva Gas Protocol 1925

The law relating to poison was formally pronounced in the 1925 Geneva Protocol for the Prohibition of the Use in War of Asphyxiating, Poisonous, or Other Gases, and Bacteriological Methods of Warfare, which prohibited the use in war of asphyxiating, poisonous, or other gases, and all analogous liquids, materials, or devices including bacteriological warfare.

Between 1925 and World War II there were no major developments in the laws of war, apart from the proposed Treaty of Paris mentioned earlier.

4.   United Nations Charter 1945

The United Nations Charter initially enacted in 1945 placed significant restrictions on the way nations can conduct themselves in terms of armed conflict. The Charter prohibits anything but self-defense in justification of conflict.

5.   Nuremberg Judgment 1946

The Judgment of the International Military Tribunal for the Trial of Major German War Criminals was delivered on 30th September and 1st October 1946. The impact of the Nuremberg Judgment is discussed elsewhere in this document. The Judgment was delivered by the Tribunal which was established by Treaty. The Treaty has annexed to it the set of legal principles to be applied, in what is known as the Nuremberg Charter.

6.   Genocide Convention 1948

After World War II the United Nations Convention on the Prevention and Punishment of the Crime of Genocide was approved by the United Nations in 1948 and adopted by the international community. It defines genocide, *inter alia*, as "the killing or causing of serious bodily or mental harm to members of a national, ethnic, racial or religious group in whole or in part."

Its intention was to protect civilian populations. It also gave rise to a concept previously elucidated at the Nuremberg Tribunal (1946), that of a crime against humanity.

The Genocide Convention was a response to Hitler's policy of exterminating German Jews, who were German citizens. The Convention seeks to ensure that if ever something like that happens again, it would no longer be considered an internal matter, but a matter subject to international law.

7.   Geneva Conventions 1949

The next developments were the Geneva Conventions of 1949, which provide protections for certain groups of people such as: wounded or sick civilians, chaplains, medical personnel, wounded or sick armed forces at sea and on land, prisoners of war and civilians. It also specified areas of protection, such as churches and medical facilities.

This was the first time civilians as a group were given specific protection, i.e., those who find themselves in case of conflict or occupation in the hands of a party to the conflict or occupying power of which they are not nationals.

8.   Nuremberg Principles 1950

The Nuremberg Principles were pronounced at the request of the General Assembly of the United Nations by the International Law Commission and adopted in a unanimous resolution in 1950. Thereafter these became rules of customary international law.

The Nuremberg Tribunal was conducted under a Charter which defined as a crime under international law, "planning, preparation, initiation or waging of a war of aggression, or a war in violation of international treaties, agreements or assurances or participation in a common plan or conspiracy for the accomplishment of any of the foregoing."

The Charter for the Nuremberg trials defined and the Judgment affirmed a number of other principles, such as Crimes against Peace, Crimes against Humanity, War Crimes and personal criminal responsibilities for the commission thereof.

9.   McCloy-Zorin Accords 1961

The McCloy-Zorin Accords was a very significant agreement, which was subsequently used as a basis for the United Nations effort to commit to a program for general and complete disarmament.

10.   Test-Ban Treaty 1963

The Test-Ban Treat of 1963 is a treaty banning nuclear weapons tests in the atmosphere, in outer space and under water, including territorial waters or high seas. Each party undertook to prohibit, to prevent, and not to carry out any nuclear weapon test or explosion, or any other nuclear explosion, at any place under its jurisdiction or control.

The parties also proclaim as their principal aim the speediest possible achievement of an agreement on general and complete disarmament.

11. Non-Proliferation Treaty 1968

The Non-Proliferation Treaty of 1968 was set up with three complementary sets of obligations:

a) Nuclear weapons states undertook not to transfer to any recipient whatsoever nuclear weapons or other nuclear explosive devices or control over such weapons or explosive devices directly, or indirectly; and not in any way to assist, encourage or induce any non-nuclear weapon state to manufacture or otherwise acquire nuclear weapons or other nuclear explosive devices, or control over such weapons or explosive devices.

b) Non-nuclear states undertook not to receive the transfer from any body of nuclear weapons or other nuclear explosive devices, or control over them, and not to manufacture or otherwise acquire nuclear weapons or other nuclear explosive devices and not to seek or receive any assistance in the manufacture of nuclear weapons or other nuclear explosive devices.

c) In addition to the prohibitions on the transfer of nuclear weapons technology, the Parties to the Treaty undertook to pursue negotiations in good faith on effective measures relating to cessation of the nuclear arms race at an early date and to nuclear disarmament, and on a treaty on general and complete disarmament under strict and effective international control.

12. Biological Weapons Convention 1972

There have since been moves to prohibit the possession of bacteriological weapons, but not the possession or manufacture of chemical weapons. The 1972 Convention Preamble also places the prohibition in the context of "achieving effective progress towards general and complete disarmament, including the prohibition and elimination of all types of weapons of mass destruction."

13. Geneva Protocols I and II 1977

In 1977 the Geneva Conventions of 1949 were amplified by

the 1977 Protocols to those Conventions.

The provisions of the 1949 Conventions were restated, greatly amplified, and extended in the Protocols by Geneva Protocol I as follows:

Article 35, section 3, says: "It is prohibited to employ methods or means of warfare which are intended, or may be expected to cause, widespread long term and severe damage to the environment."

Article 36 provides that a party to the convention is under an obligation to determine the lawfulness of the use of new weapons yet to be invented.

Article 48 provides for respect and protection of the civilian population and civilian objects, and that parties to a conflict shall distinguish between the civilian population and combatants and civilian objects and military objects and accordingly shall direct their operations only against military objectives.

Article 51 provides further protection for individual civilians and the civilian population from dangers arising from military operations.

Indiscriminate attacks are prohibited and are identified as:

a)   those not directed at a specific military objective;

b)   those which employ a method or means of combat which cannot be directed at a specific military objective, or

c)   those that employ a method or means of combat the effects of which cannot be limited as required by this protocol, and consequently are of a nature to strike military objectives and civilians or civilian objects without distinction;

d)   an attack by bombardment by any means which treats as a single military objective a number of clearly separated and distinct military objectives, located in a city, town, village or other area containing a similar concentration of civilian or civilian objects; and

e)   an attack which may be expected to cause incidental loss of life, injury to civilians, damage to civilian objects, or a combination thereof, which would be excessive in relation to the concrete and direct military advantage anticipated.

Attacks against civilian populations or civilians by way of reprisals are prohibited.

Article 52 provides general protection to civilian objects and limits attacks to military objects as defined.

Article 53 provides protection for cultural objects and places of worship.

Article 54 provides protection to objects indispensable to the survival of civilians.

Article 55 provides that:

a) "Care shall be taken in warfare to protect the natural environment against widespread long term and severe damage. This protection includes a prohibition of the use of methods or means of warfare which are intended or may be expected to cause such damage to the natural environment and thereby to prejudice the health or survival of the population";

b) "Attacks against the environment by way of reprisals are prohibited."

Article 56 provides protection against attacks on dams, dikes, and nuclear electrical generating stations even when these objectives are military objectives, "if such attack may cause the release of dangerous forces and consequent severe losses among the civilian population."

Article 59 provides that "it is prohibited for the Parties to the conflict to attack, by any means whatsoever, non-defended localities."

The Tribunal was interested to note that at the time of the 1977 Protocols, the issue was raised whether these were applicable to nuclear weapons. The earlier history of these Protocols shows that they originated from concern about the fate of civilians in nuclear war and this had been reflected by the number of Resolutions of the General Assembly of the United Nations.

In June 1977 the U.S. representative to the United Nations, Ambassador Aldrich, said: "We recognize that nuclear weapons are the subject of separate negotiations and agreements, and furthermore their use in warfare is governed by the present principles of international law."

The United States and Britain adopted a reservation to the effect that "the 1977 Protocols were not applicable to nuclear weapons." The Tribunal did however note that no such reservation was made when it came to the Geneva Conventions of 1949, even though nuclear weapons were already in existence.

14. Conventional Weapons Convention 1981

The Tribunal noted that from the beginning of the 1970s, nuclear weapons began to be excluded from the discussions at Geneva. Other meetings began and eventually led in 1981 to the "United Nations Convention on Conventional Weapons (The United Nations Convention on the Prohibition or Restriction on the Use of Certain Conventional Weapons which may be Deemed to be Excessively Injurious or to Have Indiscriminate Effects)."

This 1981 Convention does not explicitly state it is not applicable to nuclear weapons, and a consideration of the Convention terms simply reinforces the feeling that any attempt to exclude nuclear weapons from established principles of international law is merely a cynical attempt at manipulation by those involved.

Additional Treaties and Conventions

In addition to those treaties shown above there are several other treaties and conventions which have a bearing on the questions before this Tribunal. These additional treaties include the Outer Space Treaty 1967; the Latin America Nuclear Free-Zone Treaty 1967; the Vienna Convention on the Law of Treaties 1969; the Bacteriological (Biological) and Toxin Weapons Treaty 1971; the Nuclear Weapons, Sea-Bed and Ocean Floor Treaty 1971; the Anti-Ballistic Missile Treaty (SALT I) 1972; the Treaty on the Limitation of Underground Nuclear Weapons Tests 1974; the Moon Treaty 1979; and the Intermediate Nuclear Forces Treaty 1987.

Chapter 2

Unlawfulness of the Use and Possession
of Nuclear Weapons

In reality any major nuclear exchange would be an unprecedented human and environmental catastrophe proving a serious threat to the survival of all life on the planet. Even the use of a few tactical nuclear warheads would result in substantial incidental loss of civilian life and civilians would be subjected to unnecessary suffering far outweighing any immediate political or military objectives.

There are the strongest religious and moral objections to the destruction of a society through the use of nuclear weapons. Indeed, it is difficult to identify any real value system that justifies their use.

Upon the evidence, the use of nuclear weapons cannot distinguish between combatants and non-combatants, does not represent a proportionate use of force, cannot be selective or discriminating, and violates the rights of neutral nations. In short, the use of nuclear weapons is unlawful.

The question of whether mere possession of nuclear weapons is unlawful under international law is of great significance, and presents more complexities for jurisprudence than the use of nuclear weapons.

Article 6(a) of the Nuremberg Charter defines the term "crime against the peace" as "the planning, preparation, initiation or waging of a war of aggression, or a war in violation of international treaties or agreements or assurances or participation in a common plan or conspiracy, for the accomplishment of any of the foregoing."

Article 6(b) of the Nuremberg Charter defines the term "War Crimes" to include "...wanton destruction of cities, towns or villages, or devastation not justified by military necessity."

Article 6(c) of the Nuremberg Charter defines the terms "Crimes against Humanity" to include "murder, extermination, enslavement, deportation, and other inhumane acts committed against any civilian population..."

Article 6 also provides that leaders, organizers, instigators and accomplices participating in the formulation or execution of a common plan or conspiracy to commit crimes are responsible for all acts performed by any persons in execution of such plan.

Article 7 of the Nuremberg Charter demonstrates the applicability of the "act of state defense" to those who have committed such heinous crimes by making it clear that their official position "shall not be considered as freeing them from responsibility or mitigating punishment."

Article 8 of the Nuremberg Charter also provides that, although an individual may have acted pursuant to an order of his government, or of a superior, that fact should not free the individual from responsibility, but may be considered in mitigation of punishment if justice so requires.

Having stated the relevant articles, it is apparent, given the assumption that the use of nuclear weapons is unlawful, that the planning and preparation in breach of such treaties is also unlawful.

When one is considering the lawfulness of the possession of nuclear weapons, one is not considering their abstract existence. One is considering a possession of weapons whose power, speed, accuracy, deployment, and targeting taken together make it necessary for the protagonists in a potential crisis to take the nuclear initiative. In the case of the West, one is considering a declared policy to take that initiative, whether or not they are threatened with nuclear attack. The ability to manage a nuclear crisis has been reduced rather than enhanced by the development of technology. The risk of accidental or ill-judged nuclear exchange is becoming a certainty. One assesses the possession of nuclear weapons on the basis that it means possession combined with a willingness to use under certain circumstances, accidental or deliberate.

All legal systems endeavor not merely to punish crime but also to prevent it. Obviously, it is a rather ineffectual system which can only deal with crime once its effects have been felt. Accordingly, in all criminal jurisdictions intentional preparation to commit crime is itself a crime. In common law systems, one has the example of conspiracy, incitement, and attempt.

The laws of war are no exception. Thus, Article 6(a) of the Nuremberg Charter defines the term "crime against peace" as "the planning, preparation, initiation or waging of a war of aggression, or a war in violation of international treaties or agreements or assurances or participation in a common plan or conspiracy for the accomplishment of any of the foregoing." As stated above, the Article goes on to provide that leaders, organizers, instigators, and accomplices participating in the preparation or execution of a common plan or conspiracy to commit crimes against peace, crimes against humanity, and war crimes are responsible for all acts performed by any persons in execution of such a plan. Articles 7 and 8 exclude as legal defenses claims that a state has been acting in its own defense or that an individual has been following superior orders. The point is a simple one: if the consequences of the intended actions are themselves illegal, then preparation to inflict such conflict is also illegal. Whatever their disclaimers as to the use of nuclear weapons, the nuclear weapons states are expressly and by implication planning and preparing unlawful actions—the infliction of indiscriminate destruction. The development, deployment, and targeting of nuclear weapons have no other rational interpretation.

Several witnesses have dismissed the idea that nuclear weapons will never be used. Accordingly, they also dismissed the argument that what would otherwise be unlawful preparations are not so because the preparations will never in fact result in the use of nuclear weapons. On the contrary, they believe the exact opposite—that it is those very preparations which will inevitably lead to use.

Several witnesses also dismissed the alternative argument put forward by the nuclear weapons states based upon the right of self-defense contained in Article 51 of the United Nations Charter. In other words, that they are entitled under the Charter to use or at least prepare to use nuclear weapons in legitimate self-defense. It is no answer under the Charter, nor under any legal system that we know of, to say that one is merely preparing to act in self-defense where the consequences of such actions are so wholly unreasonable. It is dishonest and perverse to suggest that the unlimited and indiscriminate damage which would result from a nuclear exchange can ever be described as reasonable self-defense. The proposition offends against the entire concept of reason.

The Nuremberg Charter Articles only mention planning and

preparation. If one plans, one has an intention to act under certain circumstances, and planning with nuclear weaponry and warfare in mind is far more than an abstract idea. The war plans are developed with considerable detail; they are also adopted. This involves systems being set up for the use of the weapons and they are actually used in military maneuvers, which test the plans to ensure they actually work. The possibilities and dangers of accidental use of nuclear weapons also constitute an additional dimension of recklessness in the planning and deployment processes. Such recklessness would be considered unlawful under most legal jurisdictions of which the relevant witnesses were aware.

Professor Boyle, in his testimony to the Tribunal, held that the question of the lawfulness of states to possess nuclear weapons is itself a somewhat speculative and misdirected question, if not a misleading one. He claimed that the question may obfuscate the fact that today's acknowledged nuclear weapons states do not simply possess nuclear weapons. Rather, they actively deploy nuclear weapons in enormous numbers and varieties and attach them to delivery vehicles that are interconnected with sophisticated command, control, communication, and intelligence networks. Such nuclear weapons are ready for almost instantaneous launch upon notice. Hence, the only meaningful question for him concerns the legality of modern weapons systems as they are currently deployed and programmed for use. He suggested that if the nuclear weapons states had actually kept all their nuclear devices stored in warehouses where they were separated from their respective delivery vehicles, it might be pertinent to answer the question whether or not such mere possession of nuclear weapons was legal under international law. The nuclear weapons systems maintained by all the world's nuclear weapons states, and especially by the two superpowers, are far beyond this stage of mere possession, and have been at the point of deployment and preparation for immediate use in a thermonuclear war for quite some time. He reminded the Tribunal that under the Nuremberg Principles, such planning, preparation, and conspiracy to commit crimes against humanity, war crimes and genocide, *inter alia*, constitute international crimes in their own right.

The Tribunal feels that such defensive escalation goes beyond the level of intensity or scope permitted by the rules of target discrimination and proportionality.

The Tribunal concludes that the possession of nuclear weapons and planning of a nuclear war are in breach of Articles 6 and 6(a) of the Nuremberg Charter and the actual use of a nuclear device in all but the most remote location will be in breach of Articles 6 (b) and 6(c). An individual or organization agreeing to be part of a system which leads to the use of nuclear weapons is also in breach of the relevant Nuremberg Principles.

Following Article 8 of the Nuremberg Charter, people who obey orders may be found guilty. The Nuremberg Judgment affirms the principle that one is obliged to impede illegal action leading towards such heinous crimes, to the extent that one is able. Under such circumstances a moral choice exists whether to follow orders or not, be they civilian or military.

The General Principles of customary international law create "universality" of jurisdiction for the prosecution and punishment of those alleged to have committed heinous crimes and found guilty. All government officials and members of military forces who might order or participate in a nuclear attack upon population centers could lawfully be tried by any government of the world community that subsequently obtained control over them for the above-mentioned crimes.

Chapter 3

Judgment and Recommendations of the Tribunal

Preamble

Having considered the oral and written evidence presented during hearings and having engaged in some independent inquiry into the legal issues raised, the Tribunal has reached certain Conclusions which are embodied in this Judgment. These conclusions provide the foundation for a series of recommendations that express support for prescribed lines of action and reflect the absence of any enforcement power to assure compliance with international law on these urgent matters of nuclear weapons policy.

The conclusions as to law rest heavily on the main texts of customary and treaty international law: the 1899 and 1907 Hague Conventions on the conduct of warfare; the Martens Clause; the 1949 Geneva Conventions on humanitarian law; the two 1977 Geneva Protocols that extend the coverage of humanitarian law; the Charter of the United Nations; the Nuremberg and Tokyo judgments and the Nuremberg Principles.

Judgment

The London Nuclear Warfare Tribunal was convened in London from the 3rd to the 6th of January, 1985, for the express purpose of conducting An Examination of the Legality of Nuclear Weapons. The members of the Tribunal, having considered the oral and written evidence presented during the four days of hearings, and having engaged in independent inquiry into the legal issues raised,

DECLARE THAT

1.   Any reliance on the threat or first use of nuclear weapons is a violation of international law, and constitutes a Crime against Humanity as set forth in the Nuremberg Principle 6(c);

2.   Strategic doctrines and official war plans that contemplate first use or first strike with nuclear weapons constitute serious violations of international law, even if postures are only preparatory and contingent, and never are consummated in the form of an actual threat or use of nuclear weapons;

3.   The development, production, and deployment of nuclear weapons systems with first-strike characteristics are aggravated instances of unlawful preparations for the sake of national security, and constitute a violation of the Nuremberg prohibition on plans and conspiracies to wage aggressive war;

4.   The use of nuclear weapons in a retaliatory mode, after prior armed attack and in accordance with the concept of self-defense in the United Nations Charter, is, nevertheless, unlawful unless such use is discriminate, proportionate, and without poisonous or cruel effects; since it seems impossible to satisfy such criteria, any use of nuclear weapons, whatever the pretext or justification, is an unlawful and criminal act of war entailing both governmental and individual responsibility;

5.   As a consequence of (4), any form of deterrent threat to use nuclear weapons, even if limited to defensive and retaliatory situations, is a continuing violation of the laws of war; at minimum, overcoming deterrence with all deliberate speed is an implicit legal duty for political and military leaders representing governments of nuclear weapons states;

6.   Political and military leaders of the nuclear weapons states have also failed to fulfill the legal duty imposed by the preamble of the Limited Test Ban Treaty (1963) and Article VI of the Non-Proliferation Treaty (1968) to pursue in good faith negotiations seeking general and complete disarmament and an end to all forms of nuclear testing; the continual innovation in weapons systems, seeking maximum military advantages, has brought into being an accelerating arms race with sporadic and mainly propagandistic efforts to achieve progress toward disarmament;

7.   Currently proposed extensions of the arms race to outer space, especially in the form of the Strategic Defense Initiative (SDI), constitute separate violations of international law and appear incompatible with such existing international treaties as the Outer Space Treaty (1967), Article 1 of the Limited Test Ban Treaty (1963), and the Anti Ballistic Missile Treaty (1972);

8.   Planning and preparation for nuclear war also violate the

sovereign rights of neutral states to the extent that it causes anxiety about the harmful effects of such warfare and involves the use of weapons of mass destruction whose primary and secondary lethal effects cannot be confined to the territory of belligerent states; such violations of neutral rights are dramatized by the recent experimental indications that extensive nuclear explosions could cause "a nuclear winter" with catastrophic climatic consequences for the northern hemisphere, and possibly beyond;

9.   Planning and preparation for nuclear war undermine the development and maintenance of political democracy and constitutional government in the nuclear weapons states;

10. Any statement by any Government to the effect that the 1977 Geneva Protocols were not intended to have any effect on and do not regulate or prohibit the use of nuclear weapons, is ineffective for the purposes of avoiding criminal liability under international law for the possession or use of nuclear weapons by any State, and such statement does not reduce or eliminate individual criminal responsibility in international law for the citizens of such or other states.

On the basis of these conclusions, the Tribunal underscores the following implications.

Implications for Governments

1.   Governments are under an urgent obligation to carry out by all available means the requirements of international law as specified above, especially the governments of nuclear weapons states; above all, the United States and the Soviet Union;

2.   Governments should, in particular, initiate plans for national security that do not depend on any unlawful threat or use of nuclear weapons;

3.   Governments of non-nuclear weapons states have a particular obligation to their citizenry to pursue all lawful and political means available in international society, including recourse to the International Court of Justice, to secure compliance with international law; governments that opt for a policy of permanent neutrality have special legal standing to take action against plans and preparations for nuclear war.

Implications for Statesmen, Policy-Makers, Strategists, Advisors, Scientists, Engineers, and Military Commanders in Nuclear Weapons States and their Allies

1.   Violations of laws of war by governments entail criminal responsibility for those individuals who implement such illegal public policy by their activity, even if undertaken in the line of professional duty or pursuant to superior orders;

2.   Preparations for nuclear war and threats to use nuclear weapons involve the commission of international crimes, including Crimes against Humanity in the Nuremberg sense;

3.   Preparations to initiate nuclear war by surprise attack or through the deployment of first-strike weapons systems constitute Crimes Against Peace in the Nuremberg sense;

4.   Depending upon the overall knowledge and role of an individual, avoidance of criminal taint can be achieved only by withdrawal from all participation, direct and indirect, in criminal and unlawful activity, as well as the discharge of an affirmative duty to secure compliance with international law by all reasonable means.

Implications for Dissenters, Protesters, Resisters, and Ordinary Citizens

1.   Symbolic violations of domestic or civil law, if reasonably calculated to encourage compliance with international legal obligations pertaining to nuclear weapons, are examples of lawful disobedience, and should accordingly not be treated as punishable by courts or law enforcement officials;

2.   Citizens in all stations of life have a right and duty to implement international law even as against their own government and its officials, especially when world peace is in issue as a result of unlawful preparations for general warfare;

3.   In the event that official institutions of law on the national and international level fail to secure compliance with international law, then citizens are encouraged to constitute tribunals that operate in a fair and responsible manner to ascertain disputed matters of law and fact.

Recommendations

On the basis of this Judgment, the Tribunal believes that a series of Recommendations follow; in many instances, these recommendations are implicit in the Conclusions, but try to take some account of practical concerns, including the reality of vast arsenals of nuclear weapons and patterns of severe mistrust:

1.   The main nuclear weapons states should immediately adopt a series of provisional measures to minimize the role of nuclear weapons in national security policy; these provisional measures could include declarations of no first use, a moratorium on testing, freeze on new weapons systems, affirmation of the commitment to avoid the militarization of space, and the disavowal and dismantling of weapons with first-strike characteristics;

2.   The initiation of negotiations without preconditions and in good faith to bring national security policy into conformity with international law on matters of nuclear weapons policy as set forth in the Judgment;

3.   The initiation of negotiations without preconditions and in good faith on specific steps to achieve the verified destruction of existing stockpiles of nuclear weapons;

4.   The immediate effort to obtain a resolution within the General Assembly of the United Nations and in legal and quasi-legal bodies throughout the world to receive with approval the Judgment of this Tribunal, including its Conclusions and Recommendations;

5.   The initiation of an effort to obtain an Advisory Opinion of the International Court of Justice on the status of nuclear weapons, strategic doctrines, and war plans;

6.   The initiation of an effort to promote an international treaty that embodies the conclusions reached in the Judgment of this Tribunal;

7.   The initiation of a massive global education program on the subject matter of nuclear war and on the relevance of international law and the Nuremberg Principles to its avoidance;

8.   The initiation of a massive global effort to persuade lawyers, jurists, and their professional associations to pledge their commitment to the implementation of international law and the

Nuremberg Principles even in relation to their own government and its leaders;

9.   The organization of educational efforts along the lines of the Tribunal's Judgment geared to the specific situation of the various sectors of society, seeking especially to assure that scientists, engineers, doctors, and chaplains will not participate directly or indirectly in preparations for nuclear war;

10.   The encouragement within the sectors of various societies of a variety of forms of opposition and acts of resistance to the nuclear arms race and its manifestations, including having recourse to courts and legislatures to challenge the lawfulness of official policies;

11.   The promotion of the understanding that acts of resistance reasonably responsive to unlawful policies relating to nuclear weapons should be protected under a new doctrine of "lawful civil resistance";

12.   The acceptance worldwide by professional bodies of professional codes of conduct that state and emphasize individual and professional responsibility towards humanity when practicing any profession or trade.

Sean MacBride
Chairman of the Tribunal

Richard Falk, Dorothy Hodgkin, Maurice Wilkins
Members of the Tribunal

III.

Statement on the Illegality of Nuclear Warfare of the Lawyers Committee on Nuclear Policy

I. Introduction

With the advent of less hostile superpower relations, the opportunities for major progress toward global security and nuclear disarmament have also increased. The Intermediate Nuclear Forces Treaty (INF), while eliminating only a tiny fraction of the entire nuclear stockpile, was a major step forward in arms control. "New thinking" has overtaken traditional notions of East-West military rivalry, especially in Europe. The opening of the Berlin Wall symbolizes a new era in East-West relations.

In such a climate of hope and increased trust and understanding, leaders and citizens alike may be more disposed to consider principles of law and morality as applied to nuclear weapons.

The Lawyers Committee on Nuclear Policy believes that nuclear weapons must be abolished. We believe the use or threat of use of nuclear weapons is a grave violation of provisions of legally binding international law, and we strive to educate the legal profession and the general public about our position. To this end, we work to strengthen international legal institutions and to increase respect for international law.

Nuclear weapons still threaten all life on earth. Today's nuclear arsenals have the potential for annihilating a large segment of the world's population, for devastating and contaminating vast areas of the earth's surface, and for producing unpredictable and uncontrollable biological and environmental consequences. Among the most troubling facets of the problem are:

•   The United States, France, the United Kingdom, and NATO retain the nuclear first-use option, calling it essential to their strategy of deterrence. The other two countries which admit to having nuclear arms, the Soviet Union and the People's Republic of China, have publicly foresworn first use while retaining their capability and willingness to engage in nuclear retaliation if they are attacked first.

•   NATO and the Warsaw Pact have developed a "launch on warning" capacity, which greatly increases the danger of nuclear war by accident or miscalculation.

•   The proliferation of nuclear weapons has spread, and the need to control this spread is ever more urgent. For example, Pakistan has apparently manufactured nuclear weapons. The United States has not objected to Israel's "open secret" nuclear arsenals. The Soviet Union has assisted India's efforts to expand its nuclear weapons capability. Libyan leader Muammar Qaddafi has openly declared his interest in acquiring nuclear arms. And South Africa has a nuclear stockpile of at least fourteen and perhaps as many as twenty nuclear weapons. In Argentina, the ascension of a strong nationalist government has heightened concerns about the potential to build nuclear bombs. Brazil is moving toward a technical capability to produce nuclear bombs. North Korea signed the Non-Proliferation Treaty in 1985, but has not permitted inspectors to examine its facilities, and it has begun operating a suspiciously large research reactor and perhaps a plutonium extraction plant.

•   The Strategic Defense Initiative will enhance the first-strike capacity of the United States, and therefore threatens to unravel the entire arms control regime.

•   The continuing production of nuclear weapons creates enormous environmental hazards. The accidents and break-downs at U.S. weapons plants have dramatized the connection between nuclear weapons and environmental, health, and safety hazards. The federal government and the companies most involved in weapons production have continuously violated the public trust by ignoring or covering up these safety hazards.

•   There are far too many so-called conventional forces in the world, and these weapons are increasingly lethal. It is essential that the "smart munitions," chemical weapons, and other non-nuclear weapons of mass destruction be controlled and eventually eliminated.

•   The superpowers continue to develop newer, quicker, and more flexible nuclear weapons in an attempt to credibly threaten and, if need be, "prevail" in nuclear war. But many military and political experts agree that once begun, a nuclear war could not be contained below the level of a holocaust.

•   There have been hundreds of reported accidents involving nuclear weapons. Thousands of other incidents have gone unreported.

The last few years have seen the deployment of a new and more lethal generation of nuclear weapons; unprecedented spending on nuclear and conventional weaponry; and an attempt to reinterpret the Anti-Ballistic Missile Treaty that would permit the development of space weapons systems and effectively gut the treaty. There has been a general disregard for law in international relations, exemplified by the U.S. rejection of the World Court's jurisdiction in *Nicaragua v. United States*; by the failure of the United States to pay its U.N. dues; and by the Federal Bureau of Investigation's announced intention of seizing terrorists in foreign jurisdictions.

II.   The Law of Armed Conflict

Among the international laws of war are numerous humanitarian principles. The most basic principles of law relevant to war include that of the Just War and of the Just Conduct of War. The first analyzes the circumstances in which it is justifiable to go to war. The second analyzes, in the context of a war already underway, what constitutes just conduct of the parties involved.

The current law concerning the commencement of war is found in the U.N. Charter, article 2(4), which requires all members to refrain in their international relations from the threat or use of force against the territorial integrity or political independence of any state. The only occasion when the use of force is permissible is when a state is under armed attack, in which case the right of self-defense is recognized, within very severe limits, under article 51.

Once a war has begun, whether justly or not, the laws of Just Conduct of War are to be obeyed. These laws were first codified in the Declaration of St. Petersburg of 1868, which provided that "the right to adopt means of injuring the enemy is not unlimited," and that "the only legitimate object which States should endeavor to accomplish during a war is to weaken the military forces of the enemy," not to effect the enemy's total and irrevocable destruction. Most countries are signatories to a network of treaties in which these rules are embodied, including the Hague Convention and Regulations of 1907, and the Geneva Conventions of 1949 and the Protocols Additional of 1977. These rules are taught in military academies throughout the world and reprinted in military manuals and codes of conduct. Because of this universal acceptance, they have become part of international customary law, making them binding even on the occasional country which may not have ratified one particular treaty or another.

After the atomic bombings of Hiroshima and Nagasaki, and particularly in the last decade, a vast literature has developed concerning the applicability of the laws of war to nuclear weapons. Much of this literature has been generated by legal scholars associated with the U.S.-based Lawyers Committee on Nuclear Policy (LCNP), and the newly-founded International Association of Lawyers Against Nuclear Arms (IALANA). The modern law of Just Conduct of War can be summarized in six rules, which are generally accepted and considered binding by the vast majority of countries. Under these rules:

1.   It is prohibited to use weapons or tactics that cause indiscriminate harm as between combatants and noncombatants, and military and civilian personnel.

Evidence from major pre-Christian cultures suggests that the use of a military weapon which would destroy the entire population of an enemy was prohibited. Early Hindu, Chinese, and Jewish legal texts laid the groundwork for European development of this rule after the thirteenth century. The International Committee of the Red Cross stated in its commentary on the 1949 Geneva Conventions that "the civilian population can never be regarded as a military objective." The principle of target discrimination became an essential part of the Hague Draft Rules on Aerial Warfare of 1923. The universally binding Geneva Conventions of 1949 updated and greatly strengthened this rule. The Convention on the Protection of Civilian Persons in Time of War imposes detailed obligations on all belligerents to ensure the health, safety, and sustenance of the civilian populations.

2.   It is prohibited to use weapons or tactics that cause unnecessary or aggravated devastation and suffering.

Fundamental to the prohibition of inflicting suffering *per se* is the view that such tactics violate the laws of humanity and do not further the purposes of war. This prohibition was specifically ratified in the Declaration of St. Petersburg in 1868. The treaty banned the use of exploding bullets, and it created a general prohibition against any weapons "which uselessly aggravated the sufferings of disabled men, or render their death inevitable." Such methods of warfare are also "especially prohibited" by the Regulations embodied in the Hague Convention IV of 1907. The U.S. Air Force views the Hague Conventions as a central component of the modern Law of Armed Conflict.

These limitations have been developed further in subsequent decades, especially in the wake of the unparalleled cruelty of World Wars I and II. A lawful war must defeat the enemy with the least expenditure of time, life, and resources. A war is outlawed if it terrorizes the civilian population, delays the enemy's postwar recovery, or destroys the enemy altogether. These principles are restated in various manuals published by the armed forces of the United States.

3.   It is prohibited to use weapons or tactics that violate the neutral jurisdiction of non-participating countries.

This principle has been well-established in treaty law since at least the Hague Conventions of 1907. Belligerent states must not carry their hostilities—including radioactive fallout from nuclear war—into the territory of non-participating states.

4.   It is prohibited to use asphyxiating, poisonous, or other gases, and all analogous liquids, materials, or devices.

The Geneva Gas Protocol of 1925 establishes this ban. It applies to chemical weapons and "all analogous liquids, materials, or devices," which, by any reasonable interpretation, would include nuclear devices. The United States became a party to the treaty in 1975.

5.   It is prohibited to use weapons or tactics that cause widespread, long-term, and severe damage to the environment.

The growing understanding that human beings are part of a complex web of life has helped bolster the idea that destruction of the environment, e.g., nuclear winter, is an international crime. This rule was added to the international laws of war by the 1977 Protocol I Additional to the 1949 Geneva Conventions.

6.   It is prohibited to effect reprisals that are disproportionate to their provocation.

The ban on reprisals that exceed their provocation, or are undertaken for punitive or vengeful purposes, dates back to the laws of chivalry and even earlier sources. In the modern context, disproportionate warfare violates, *inter alia*, article 35 (1) of the 1977 Protocol Additional to the 1949 Geneva Conventions.

This rule has a very special position in the laws of war. If a belligerent army violates any one of rules 1-5, the opposing army is thereby justified in retaliating proportionally. However, this justification is limited to reprisals which de-escalate a military conflict. A warring nation may retaliate for grave and manifestly unlawful acts, but should not destroy persons, institutions, or resources otherwise protected by the laws of war. The response must be proportionate to the original violation.

Furthermore, reprisals must in all other respects be carried out in observance of international law. Reprisals must be directed at the co-belligerent state with no adverse impact upon the territory or the people of neutral countries and must otherwise comply with the rules of discrimination. Reprisals are prohibited when directed at civilian populations, prisoners of war, against wounded and sick military or civilian persons, medical personnel, cultural institutions and landmarks, places of worship, dams, dikes, and nuclear power generators.

Each of these six principle humanitarian rules of warfare involves a balancing of the customary principle of humanity against the doctrine of military necessity. Though somewhat eroded over the years and obviously susceptible to evasive interpretation, these traditional humanitarian rules continue to be a vital civilizing influence upon the world community's warring propensities. They are endowed with an authority that makes them applicable to nuclear as well as to conventional weapons and warfare.

Restraints on the conduct of hostilities are traditionally not limited to those given explicit voice in specific treaty stipulations. Aware of the continuous evolution of war technology, the 1907 Hague Convention IV contains a general yardstick intended exactly for situations where no specific treaty rule exists to prohibit a new type of weapon or tactic. This general rule, known as the Martens Clause, provides that, in cases not covered by the Regulations, "the inhabitants and the belligerents remain under the protection and the rule of the principles of the law of nations as they result from the usages established among civilized peoples, from the laws of humanity and the dictates of public conscience." No new treaty specifically prohibiting a new weapon is necessary.

III.   Is the Use of Nuclear Weapons Illegal?

Almost every use to which nuclear weapons might be put, most notably the standard strategic and theater-level options which dominate United States and Soviet nuclear policy, violates one or more of the laws of war.

The cardinal principle of *proportionality* (number 6) is the most clearly violated rule. A nuclear war of "assured destruction" would make a mockery of this key principle. Once a massive nuclear attack is launched, all conceptions of proportionality become meaningless.

Even the so-called "defensive" use of "smart" nuclear weapons is a violation of the proportionality doctrine. Strategists argue that these weapons could be used to respond to a massive conventional attack in a "battlefield" situation. But flexible nuclear weapons and strategies represent a deliberate and illegal escalation of hostilities.

Nuclear war also violates the prohibition against *causing unnecessary and aggravated devastation and suffering* (rule 2). And obviously, the use of nuclear weapons would violate the ban on *indiscriminate harm to combatants and non-combatants* (rule 1). In any nuclear war, a very slight fraction of the dead would be soldiers. Cities and regions with large civilian populations would be targeted. The resulting annihilation of entire population groups would clearly violate the discrimination principle.

In fact, all-out nuclear war would violate the Genocide Treaty, since it would be aimed at the destruction of entire ethnic groups, peoples, or nations. And even if a nuclear war somehow could be limited to industrial, military, or command and communications installations of an adversary, such a war would still be unlawful, since the majority of these so-called "military targets" are located in or near urban population centers.

The use of "battlefield" nuclear weapons in Europe would also fail the discrimination test of international law. Such a "battle" would surely strike close to urban areas with dense populations, resulting in millions of civilian casualties. And, once the nuclear firebreak was crossed, one side or both would be likely to resort to an all-out response.

Given the uncontainable nature of radiation, nuclear war also violates the *neutrality* principle (rule 3). Many neutral countries would be necessarily downwind of belligerent countries subjected to nuclear attack. Any country that decides to engage in a major nuclear war is deliberately drawing in other nations not involved in the conflict. Even a so-called "limited" nuclear war would have devastating impacts on non-participating countries.

Nuclear war could destroy the entire ecosystem and all of humanity with it. A new legal and moral concept has been developed to characterize this possibility: omnicide, or the extinction of all life.

On the basis of these fundamental principles, the United Nations has repeatedly condemned the use of nuclear weapons as an "international crime." On November 24, 1961, the General

Assembly declared in Resolution 1653 (XVI) that "any state using nuclear or thermonuclear weapons is to be considered as violating the Charter of the United Nations, as acting contrary to the law of humanity, and as committing a crime against mankind and civilization." In a series of subsequent resolutions, the General Assembly has declared that the use or threat of use of nuclear weapons would be a violation of the Charter of the United Nations and a crime against humanity. These resolutions demonstrate an emerging global consensus that nuclear weapons violate, in the words of the Martens Clause, "the laws of humanity and the dictates of public conscience."

If the use of nuclear weapons is illegal, did the atomic bombings of Hiroshima and Nagasaki constitute crimes against humanity or war crimes as defined by the Nuremberg Charter of August 8, 1945?

The leading authority on this point is the *Shimoda* case, decided by the District Court of Tokyo, on December 7, 1963. The plaintiffs, Japanese nationals, were all residents of either Hiroshima or Nagasaki when atomic bombs were dropped on these cities by the United States Air Force in August 1945.

The *Shimoda* court ruled that the bombings were illegal. Among other reasons, the court held that the atomic weapons produced *unnecessary and cruel forms of suffering*, in violation of the laws of war.

IV.   Is the Threat of Use of Nuclear Weapons Illegal?

If a given use of nuclear weapons is judged to be contrary to the humanitarian rules of armed conflict, then logically any threat of such use should be considered contrary to the humanitarian rules of armed conflict as well. This is supported by general principles of law concerning "inchoate crimes" (involving, for example, threats and conspiracies to commit unlawful acts), as well as basic notions of moral philosophy.

Article 2(4) of the Charter of the United Nations prohibits "the threat or use of force against the territorial integrity or political independence of any state, or in any other manner inconsistent with the purposes of the United Nations." Any use of a "clean" tactical nuclear weapon, assuming such a thing were possible, would not be effective as a deterrent. On the other hand, strategic or theater-level nuclear war would most likely destroy the territorial integrity and political independence of a target state, and it would be inconsistent with other purposes of the United Nations, such as preserving the right to life, safeguarding the environment, etc. Therefore, the threat of use of nuclear weapons as a deterrent constitutes a violation of article 2(4).

What kinds of threats are prohibited? A clearly articulated official communique credibly indicating a nuclear attack if certain demands are not met likely falls within the zone of prohibition. By the same token, even the commonplace advance preparation of nuclear missiles for immediate launch, as happens periodically in actual or perceived crises, is unlawful.

What about the entire remaining continuum of nuclear threats: ranging from legislative appropriation and research and development to manufacture, stockpiling and deployment of warheads and delivery systems? Are these likewise susceptible to suppositions of illegality?

Proponents of the strategy known as deterrence argue that the goals of preventing and deterring nuclear war resound in article 51 of the U.N. Charter, which safeguards "the inherent right of individual or collective self-defense" in case of an "armed attack."

However, the right of self-defense is not unlimited, and deterrence is an illusory strategy. The essence of the deterrence doctrine is that each side must believe that the other side's capability is actual, and that its will to use nuclear weapons is unswerving. Deterrence then becomes not the storage of weapons with intent to terrify, but a stockpiling with *intent to use*, which brings it within the ambit of the prohibitions applicable to *use* of the weapon. Therefore, it is clear that nuclear deterrence violates the laws of war, at least insofar as it entails an imminent possibility of use.

The unlawfullness and immorality of nuclear deterrence are also demonstrated by considering other threats which have the alleged purpose of preserving the peace. Such deterrent threats can be seen as violating the basic principles which underlie international humanitarian law. Humanitarian law recognizes that war will occur, but limits the permissible methods for waging war. On the other hand, deterrence attempts to eliminate conflict through the threat of a war waged by illegal means. It is immoral and illegal for a state to imply its willingness to violate principles of humanitarian law to impose substantial and unacceptable costs on any potential adversary.

Many legal scholars support this conclusion. Some take the argument further: nuclear weapons are by their very nature illegitimate, because their use cannot be controlled or their effects limited. Therefore, the research, manufacture, possession, transportation, deployment, and testing of these weapons must be unlawful as well.

Three additional aspects of the deterrence system are most troubling from an international law perspective:

• *Counter-ethnic targeting.* According to independent sources, strategists in the Carter administration developed nuclear war plans incorporating a philosophy known as "counter-ethnic targeting." In other words, major population centers inhabited primarily by members of certain ethnic groups were selected for repeated and especially severe nuclear destruction because of their constituent ethnicity alone. Whatever the alleged political justification for this practice, all government officials involved in the nuclear targeting of ethnic groups would be committing the international crime of conspiracy to commit genocide, as defined by articles 1, 2, 3, and 4 of the 1948 Genocide Convention.

• *Counter-city targeting.* A nuclear attack by a state upon another state's civilian population centers is absolutely prohibited under all circumstances, even if undertaken in retaliation for a prior attack against the first state's civilian population centers.

• *First-strike weapons and contingency plans.* A surprise, pre-emptive nuclear strike by one country against another would be a war of aggression, absolutely prohibited under international law. Consequently, all first-strike strategic nuclear weapons as well as their concommitant command, control and communications systems and first-strike contingency plans are prohibited, illegal, and criminal.

Contingency planning for a nuclear first-strike would be illegal even in response to an overwhelming conventional attack. The devastating capacity of nuclear arsenals makes a proportional and discriminating nuclear response to a conventional attack impossible. Consequently, the planning of any type of first strike would clearly be in violation of the laws of war.

In sum, deterrence must be replaced with international legal institutions to safeguard the peace without threatening it.

V.   The Constitution and Domestic Law

The United States Constitution does not refer specifically to the problems and challenges posed by nuclear weapons. But the framers' vision of a "right to life, liberty, and the pursuit of happiness" cannot be reconciled with the prospect of nuclear annihilation.

The narrow constitutional authority of the Executive to defend the country against an attack does not include the power to enormously escalate the conflict by resorting to the first use of nuclear weapons. Article VI, Clause 2, of the Constitution specifies that international law "shall be the supreme law of the land." The President has the duty to execute that law and not contravene it. Therefore, the President has the duty to obey and enforce international law, and the first use of nuclear weapons violates that obligation.

Moreover, the present hair-trigger nuclear strategy deprives Congress of its constitutionally mandated right and prerogative to decide and declare when the country should go to war (Article I, Section 8, Clause 11). Congress never delegated its power over nuclear weapons to the President, nor can it. Congress should legislate to reassert its authority in this area.

Indeed, if the use or threat of use of nuclear weapons is illegal under international law, U.S. courts must have jurisdiction to address the problem. Until now, U.S. courts have generally surrendered this jurisdiction by using the "political question" doctrine as a self-imposed limitation of power.

Nuclear weapons have also become an excuse for the Executive Branch and the military to override requirements of domestic law. For example:

• The military operates in virtual secrecy, free of public scrutiny or accountability. The Department of Energy consistently lied about the degree of radioactive hazards present at weapons production plants at Savannah River in South Carolina and Hanford in Washington state. Also, the Navy has built "homeports" for nuclear-equipped ships in the harbors of major cities on three coasts without confirming or denying that the weapons will be onboard the ships. This is all the more troubling given the hundreds of accidents that have occurred with nuclear weapons.

• Courts have created huge "national security" exceptions for nuclear weapons programs to the National Environmental Protection Act and other statutes. The United States has not yet fully addressed the environmental implications of its weapons arsenal. We will be dealing with the radioactive waste from nuclear weapons production for thousands of years, and there is probably no way to "clean up" the hazards at the many sites around the country.

• The Department of Energy does not effectively protect the public health and safety as it relates to nuclear weapons production. The same agencies of the federal government run the nuclear weapons program and regulate it. Therefore, the environment and the welfare of people near weapons plants are not protected as effectively as they might be if the states and municipalities were involved.

VI. Conclusion: The Growth of Law and the Responsibility of Lawyers

How is law to be used in the search for nuclear disarmament? First, we—and that means all of us, lawyers and non-lawyers—must know and say what the law is. It cannot be right that the great powers, the nuclear powers, should continue to proclaim their adherence to the rule of law while basing their strategic doctrines on nuclear deterrence, which is illegal and perhaps criminal.

Second, we must get judges, most of whom are either ignorant or wary of the elementary principles of international law, to say what the law is. There are many ways to do this: IALANA, for instance, in cooperation with the International Physicians for the Prevention of Nuclear War, is pursuing a project to seek an advisory opinion from the World Court on the legal status of nuclear weapons. A group of Canadian lawyers and activists are planning to raise in their courts the question whether Canada can remain a member of NATO as long as NATO's strategy is based on nuclear deterrence. Prior to the enactment of the INF Treaty, German, Belgian and Dutch peace groups brought actions in their respective courts challenging the deployment of intermediate range missiles. The women of Greenham Common did the same in U.S. courts. In the United States, international law defenses to protests against illegal foreign or defense policies are still generally rejected, but are beginning to be accepted by a growing minority of judges.

Third, a deliberate effort must be made to fill in the lacunae in the current international law doctrine by enacting laws and treaties creating nuclear-free zones and prohibiting the development, deployment, and possession of nuclear weapons, even if only in a manner confirmatory of the already existing principles of international law.

Lawyers have a critical role to play in creating a world that is both non-nuclear and non-violent. The past four decades have seen a proliferation of human rights laws, dealing with subjects as diverse as torture, disappearance, summary executions, and social and economic rights. The time has now come to proclaim the most fundamental right of all, the right to peace. Without this right, in a world teetering on the brink of extinction, all other rights have no meaning.

The right to life, enshrined in the Universal Declaration of Human Rights and our own Declaration of Independence, means more than the freedom of an individual from arbitrary murder by the state. It means the right of the world's people to realize the possibility for development, to be confident of our own survival and the survival of our children, and to live on a habitable planet.

We face the challenge of developing remedies for government practices which no longer reflect accepted norms of morality and legality. It is in performing this healing function that lawyers can exercise their unique skills as reformers of domestic and world legal processes and make an important contribution to the resolution of society's greatest problems.

The law alone will not bring about that monumental achievement, just as the law would not, by itself, have brought an end to the divine right of kings, slavery, child labor, exclusive male suffrage, racial discrimination, or the Vietnam War. But social progress with respect to these and many other issues would not have occurred without the intervention of legal principles in the political debate, or the confirmation of changing values in the form of legal principles. So too, in the context of the existence of nuclear weapons, lawyers and legal principles should lead the way in forging consensus, this time among peoples divided by culture and geography, yet united by common interest in continued survival and world peace.

IV.

The Hague Declaration on the Illegality of Nuclear Weapons of the International Association of Lawyers Against Nuclear Arms (IALANA)

(adopted at the IALANA General Assembly
on September 24, 1989)

The International Association of Lawyers Against Nuclear Arms (IALANA) was founded in Stockholm in April 1988. It is the only international organization of lawyers devoted to applying legal skills and principles to the struggle to prevent a nuclear holocaust and rid the world of nuclear weapons.

Member organizations of IALANA include:

Association of Soviet Lawyers
Australian Lawyers for Nuclear Disarmament
Dutch Association of Lawyers for Peace
Finnish Lawyers' Peace Committee
Indian Lawyers Against Nuclear Arms
Judges and Prosecutors for Peace, West Germany
Juristen tegen Kernwapens, Belgium
Jurister for Fred, Denmark
Juristes Contre L'Arme Nucleaire, France
Lawyers Committee on Nuclear Policy, U.S.A.
Lawyers for the Elimination of Nuclear Weapons, Japan
Lawyers for Nuclear Disarmament, Britain

New Zealand Lawyers for Nuclear Disarmament
Norske Jurister mot Atomvapen, Norway
Palestinian Lawyers Union
Swedish Lawyers Against Nuclear Arms
Vietnam Lawyers Organization

The International Association of Lawyers Against Nuclear Arms (IALANA), meeting at its First World Congress at The Hague, September 22-24, 1989,

concerned about the continuation of the nuclear arms race and the maintenance of military strategies based on the use of omnicidal weapons;

calling attention to United Nations General Assembly Resolution 39/11 of November 12, 1984, on the Right of Peoples to Peace;

rejecting strongly any argument that the use or the threat of use of nuclear weapons is permitted because they are nowhere expressly prohibited as such;

convinced that such a suggestion conflicts directly with the Martens Clause first mentioned in The Hague Convention of 1899 with Respect to the Laws and Customs of War on Land and subsequently restated in other universally binding instruments of international law, which clause states that

> in cases not included in the Regulations...populations and belligerents remain under the protection and empire of the principles of international law, as they result from the usages established between civilized nations, from the laws of humanity, and the requirements of the public conscience;

affirming that the use or threat of use of nuclear weapons is a war crime and a crime against humanity as well as a gross violation of other norms of international customary and treaty law;

envisioning as an urgent task the total outlawing of nuclear

weapons, including their research, manufacturing, and possession;

stressing the primacy of international law, and;

convinced that the peoples and nations of the world must for
their survival submit themselves to the rule of law in international affairs;

welcoming the Hague Declaration of the Ministers of Foreign
Affairs of the Movement of the Non-Aligned Countries Meeting
to Discuss the Issues of Peace and the Rule of Law in International Affairs in June 1989, approved by the non-aligned summit
in Belgrade in September 1989, which calls on the United
Nations General Assembly to declare a Decade of Peace and
International Law in order to realize the hope for a peaceful
world with justice for all;

urges legal and other non-governmental organizations throughout the world to support the above mentioned initiative of the
non-aligned states;

invites lawyers throughout the world to sensitize "the public
conscience" to the incompatibility of nuclear weapons with
international law and to utilize their respective legal processes
to build up a body of law dealing with various aspects of the
problem;

calls upon all Governments to conduct their international relations and their military planning in accordance with the mandates of the United Nations Charter, especially Article 2(4), and
the laws of war and other relevant principles and rules of
international law, including those relating to the rights of
neutral states, the rights to life, peace and development, genocide, the environment, self-determination, non-intervention,
and other human and peoples' rights;

More specifically, IALANA

appeals to the Governments of all Member States of the United

Nations to take immediate steps toward obtaining a resolution by the United Nations Assembly under Article 96 of the United Nations Charter, requesting the International Court of Justice to render an advisory opinion on the illegality of the use of nuclear weapons;

dedicates itself to the enunciation and promotion of the rights to life and to peace as the most fundamental of all human rights, in accordance with the United Nations Charter, Articles 3 and 28 of the Universal Declaration of Human Rights, and Article 6 of the International Convention on Civil and Political Rights and General Comments 6(16) and 14(23) of the Human Rights Committee of the United Nations;

pledges to undertake a major effort to bring about a re-examination of the myth of nuclear deterrence as keeper of the peace;

supports the worldwide movement toward the establishment of nuclear-free zones and the right of the people at all levels, municipal, national, and regional, to establish such zones;

offers to work with the International Physicians for the Prevention of Nuclear War and other organizations for a Comprehensive Test Ban;

believes the disarmament negotiations must not only deal with existing weapons, but must focus on stopping the development and introduction of new arms technologies relating to all weapons of mass destruction;

considers that, quite apart from the legal, moral, strategic, and political aspects of nuclear weapons, the harmful consequences of their production are incompatible with the peoples' right to health and to a clean environment;

requests nuclear weapons states adhere to the Nuclear Nonproliferation Treaty;

expresses its deep concern with the continuing sufferings of the Hibakusha and its sympathy with the Appeal from Hiroshima and Nagasaki for a Total Ban and Elimination of Nuclear Weapons, and;

calls on Governments to seize the present historic opportunity to reverse the arms race and utilize the resources thus made available for the task of achieving these ends.

Notes

Introduction by Burns H. Weston

1.   Address before a Joint Session of Congress on the Persian Gulf Crisis and the Federal Budget Deficit, Sept. 11, 1990, 26 WEEKLY COMP. PRES. DOC. 1358, 1359 (Sept. 17, 1990); *Confrontation in the Gulf: Telling it on Capitol Hill; Text of President Bush's Address to Joint Session of Congress*, N.Y. Times, Sept. 12, 1990, at A10, col. 1.
2.   *See generally,* Weston, *The Reagan Administration Versus International Law*, 19 CASE W. RES. J. INT'L L. 295 (1987). *See also* Malawer, *Reagan's Law and Foreign Policy, 1981-1987: The "Reagan Corollary" of International Law*, 29 HARV. INT'L L. J. 85 (1988). *Cf.* Beres, *Ignoring International Law: U.S. Policy on Insurgency and Intervention in Central America*, 14 DEN. J. INT'L L. & POL'Y 76 (1985); Highet, *Remarks by Keith Highet as President of the American Society of International Law at the 1987 Annual Banquet of the Society held on April 10, 1987 in Boston, Massachusetts*, 81 AM. SOC'Y INT'L L. PROC. 501 (1987); Kreisberg, *Does the U.S. Government Think That International Law Is Important?*, 11 YALE J. INT'L L. 479 (1986); Quigley, *The Reagan Administration's Legacy to International Law*, 2 TEMPLE INT'L & COMP. L. J. 199 (1989). For a more general treatment, see Farer, *International Law: The Critics Are Wrong*, 71 FOR. POL'Y 22 (Summer 1988).
3.   See EINSTEIN ON PEACE 632-35 (O. Nathan & H. Norden eds., 1968).
4.   The reader is requested to construe the masculine gender

used in this extract in the generic sense, to include women as well as men.

5.   See, e.g., INTERNATIONAL PHYSICIANS FOR THE PREVENTION OF NUCLEAR WAR, LAST AID: THE MEDICAL DIMENSIONS OF NUCLEAR WAR (1982); National Council of Catholic Bishops, *Pastoral Letter on War and Peace—The Challenge of Peace: God's Promise and Our Response,* 13 ORIGINS No. 1 (May 19, 1983) *reprinted in part in* TOWARD NUCLEAR DISARMAMENT AND GLOBAL SECURITY 123 (B. Weston ed., 1984). *See also* THE FINAL EPIDEMIC: PHYSICIANS AND SCIENTISTS ON NUCLEAR WAR (R. Adams & S. Cullen eds., 1981); J. SCHELL, THE FATE OF THE EARTH (1982).

6.   Now known as "Lawyers Alliance for World Security" (LAWS), headquartered at 1120 19th Street, N.W., Suite 615, Washington, D.C. 20036. Incorporated in 1981 as the Lawyers Alliance for Nuclear Arms Control (LANAC), LAWS is a nonpartisan, educational association of legal professionals, including leading figures with a variety of political views. LAWS conducts programs that seek to reduce the threat and likelihood of the use of weapons of mass destruction, especially nuclear weapons. These programs include the Lawmaking for Democracy Project, the LAWS Right to Know Project, the LAWS Minimum Deterrence Project, and the LAWS Non-Proliferation Project.

7.   Headquartered at 666 Broadway, 6th Floor, New York, N.Y. 10012. Building on the experience of the Lawyers Committee on American Policy Towards Vietnam [see, *e.g.,* VIETNAM AND INTERNATIONAL LAW: AN ANALYSIS OF INTERNATIONAL LAW AND THE USE OF FORCE, AND THE PRECEDENT OF VIETNAM FOR SUBSEQUENT INTERVENTIONS (Northampton, MA: Aletheia Press, 1990), originally published as VIETNAM AND INTERNATIONAL LAW: THE ILLEGALITY OF UNITED STATES MILITARY INVOLVEMENT (1967)], the Lawyers Committee on Nuclear Policy borrowed from the successes of the medical profession's raising of the health aspects of nuclearism under the leadership of the Physicians for Social Responsibility and the International Physicians for Social Responsibility, the latter winning the Nobel Peace Prize.

8.   It is true, of course, that not all legal scholars agree with this

finding. *See, e.g.,* Almond, *Deterrence and A Policy-Oriented Perspective on the Legality of Nuclear Weapons,* in NUCLEAR WEAPONS AND LAW 75 (A. Miller & M. Feinreider eds., 1984); Moore, *Nuclear Weapons and the Law: Enhancing Strategic Stability, id.* at 51; Reisman, *Deterrence and International Law, id.* at 129. *See also* Lisle, Remarks: *Nuclear Weapons—A Conservative Approach to Treaty Interpretation,* 9 BROOKLYN J. INT'L L. 275 (1983); Rostow, *Is There a Legal Basis for Nuclear Deterrence Theory and Policy?,* in LAWYERS AND THE NUCLEAR DEBATE—PROCEEDINGS OF THE CANADIAN CONFERENCE ON NUCLEAR WEAPONS AND THE LAW 175 (M. Cohen & M. Gouin eds. 1988). However, the preponderance of scholarly opinion on the use and threat of use of nuclear weapons clearly favors this view. See, e.g., C. BUILDER & M. GRAUBARD, THE INTERNATIONAL LAW OF ARMED CONFLICT: IMPLICATIONS FOR THE CONCEPT OF ASSURED DESTRUCTION (Rand Publication Series R-28044-FF, 1982); F. KALSHOVEN, CONSTRAINTS ON THE WAGING OF WAR (1987); E. MEYROWITZ, PROHIBITION OF NUCLEAR WEAPONS: THE RELEVANCE OF INTERNATIONAL LAW (1990); B. ROLING: THE IMPACT OF NUCLEAR WEAPONS ON INTERNATIONAL RELATIONS AND INTERNATIONAL LAW (1982); G. SCHWARZENBERGER, THE LEGALITY OF NUCLEAR WEAPONS (1958); N. SINGH, NUCLEAR WEAPONS AND INTERNATIONAL LAW (1959); J. SPAIGHT, THE ATOMIC PROBLEM (1948); C. WEERAMANTRY, NUCLEAR WEAPONS AND SCIENTIFIC RESPONSIBILITY (1987); Arbess, *The International Law of Armed Conflict in Light of Contemporary Deterrence Strategies: Empty Promises or Meaningful Restraint?,*30 MCGILL L. J. 89 (1984); Boyle, *The Relevance of International Law to the "Paradox" of Nuclear Deterrence,* 80 NW. U. L. REV. 1407 (1986); Brownlie, *Some Legal Aspects of the Use of Nuclear Weapons,* 14 INT'L & COMP. L. Q. 437 (1965); Castren, *The Illegality of Nuclear Weapons,* 3 U. TOL. L. REV. 89 (1971); Corwin, *The Legality of Nuclear Arms Under International Law,* 5 DICKINSON J. INT'L L. 271 (1987); Falk, Meyrowitz & Sanderson, *Nuclear Weapons and International Law,* 20 INDIANA J. INT'L L. 541 (1980); Fried, *International Law Prohibiting the First Use of Nuclear Weapons: Existing Prohibitions in International Law,* 12 BULL. PEACE PRO-

POSALS 21 (1981); Fried, *The Nuclear Collision Course: Can International Law Be of Help?*, 14 DEN. J. INT'L. L. & POL'Y 97 (1985); Fujita, *First Use of Nuclear Weapons: Nuclear Strategy vs. International Law*, 3 KANSAI U. REV. L. & POL. 57 (1982); Fujita, *Status of Nuclear Weapons in International Law*, 7 KANSAI U. REV. L. & POL. 1 (1986); Kennedy, *A Critique of United States Nuclear Deterrence Theory*, 9 BROOKLYN J. INT'L. L. 35 (1983); Lippman, *Nuclear Weapons and International Law: Towards a Declaration on the Prevention and Punishment of the Crime of Nuclear Humanicide*, 8 LOY. L. A. INT'L & COMP. L. ANN. 183 (1986); McGrath, *Nuclear Weapons: The Crisis of Conscience*, 107 MIL. L. REV. 191 (1985); H. Meyrowitz, *Les juristes devant l'arme nucleaire*, 67 REV. GEN. INT'L PUB. 820 (1963); Nanda, *Nuclear Weapons and the Right to Peace Under International Law: A Fundamental Challenge*, 9 BROOKLYN J. INT'L L. 283 (1982); Pogany, *Nuclear Weapons and Self-Defense in International Law: An Emerging Standard for a Nuclear Age*, 59 N.Y.U.L. REV. 187 (1984); Polebaum, *National Self-Defense in International Law: An Emerging Standard for a Nuclear Age*, 59 N.Y.U.L. REV. 187 (1984); Ragone, *The Applicability of Military Necessity in the Nuclear Age*, 16 N.Y.U.J. INT'L L. & POL. 701 (1984); Rosas, *Negative Security and Non-Use of Nuclear Weapons*, 25 GERMAN Y. B. INT'L L. 199 (1982); Rubin, *Nuclear Weapons and International Law*, 8 FLETCHER FORUM 45 (1984); For a useful overview, see E. Meyrowitz, *The Opinions of Legal Scholars on the Legal Status of Nuclear Weapons*, 24 STAN. J. INT'L L. 111 (1987).

9.   For information regarding the formation of the Federation of Earth Provisional District World Court, see Leon Vickman's Preface to this book, p. ix.

10.   Due to the initiative of several British organizations (Architects for Peace, Campaign for Nuclear Disarmament, the Green Party, Haldane Society of Socialist Lawyers, Journalists Against Nuclear Extermination, Medical Campaign Against Nuclear Weapons, National Peace Council, National Union of Public Employees, Scientists Against Nuclear Arms, Scottish Lawyers for Nuclear Disarmament, the Quaker Society of Friends, Teachers for Peace, and the United Nations Association) and many individuals, a Nuclear Warfare Tribunal was established that would sit in London to hear evidence and arguments on the

legality of nuclear weapons. Sean MacBride presided over the Tribunal, and Richard Falk, Dorothy Hodgkin, and Maurice Wilkins served as judges. The Tribunal proceedings took place on January 2-6, 1985.

11. *See supra* note 7.

12. The International Association of Lawyers Against Nuclear Arms (IALANA) was established on April 8 and 9, 1988, when prominent lawyers from eleven countries (the United States, the Soviet Union, Great Britain, Sweden, Australia, Japan, Finland, the Federal Republic of Germany, the German Democratic Republic, Yugoslavia, and The Netherlands) gathered in Stockholm, Sweden. The intention to establish IALANA was announced jointly in August 1987 in New York City by the Lawyers Committee on Nuclear Policy (U.S.A.) and the Association of Soviet Lawyers at the International Conference on Nuclear Weapons and International Law. IALANA takes the position that the use or threat of use of nuclear weapons violates international law and constitutes a crime against humanity and peace. IALANA's ultimate goal is an international legal system in which inter-state disputes will be settled peacefully and without the use or threatened use of violence. For additional information on IALANA's activities, write the Lawyers Committee on Nuclear Policy, 666 Broadway, 6th Floor, New York, NY 10012.

13. *See* Article 38 (1)(d) of the Statute of the International Court of Justice, June 26, 1945, 59 Stat. 1031, T.S. No. 993, 3 Bevans 1153, 1976 Y.B.U.N. 1052, *reprinted in* BASIC DOCUMENTS IN INTERNATIONAL LAW AND WORLD ORDER 33 (B. Weston, R. Falk, A. D'Amato eds., 2d ed., 1990) (hereinafter "BASIC DOCUMENTS").

14. Thus, for example, did syndicated columnist Cal Thomas write three weeks after the commencement of "Operation Desert Storm":

> The United States should use tactical nuclear weapons against Iraqi forces occupying Kuwait to bring the Persian Gulf War to a speedy conclusion and thereby save lives of American and allied fighters….Better to end the cruelty as rapidly as possible once war has begun. Better to enhance the possibility of a rapid conclusion by using tactical nuclear weapons now.

Thomas, The Way to Deal with Iraq: Nuke It, Des Moines

Register, Feb. 7, 1991, at 8A. See also, Goodman, Nuke's Appeal to U.S. Public is Chilling, Des Moines Register, Feb. 15, 1991, at 8A; Heard, Brat PAC: Among the Conservative Weenies; Conservative Political Action Conference, 204 NEW REPUBLIC 15 (Mar. 4, 1991).

15.   U.N.G.A. Res. S-10/2 (S-X), 10 (Special) U.N. GAOR, Supp. (No. 4) 3, U.N. Doc A/S-10/4 (1978), *reprinted in* BASIC DOCUMENTS at 253.

16.   *See Conference on Disarmament*, U.N. Doc. CD/549 (Feb. 6, 1985), reprinted in BASIC DOCUMENTS at 273.

17.   *See* ALTERNATIVE SECURITY: LIVING WITHOUT NUCLEAR DETERRENCE 78 (B. Weston ed., 1990) (hereinafter "ALTERNATIVE SECURITY").

18.   *See* Weston, *Law and Alternative Security: Toward a Just World Peace*, in ALTERNATIVE SECURITY, at 78. The ensuing discussion is abridged and revised from this essay. Readers wishing greater detail should consult the original essay and the larger collection from which it is derived. Such consultation is desirable because it will underscore the fact that there is no such thing as a strictly *legal* alternative or set of alternatives to nuclear deterrence. Nuclear weapons are weapons of military decisiveness. Any substitute for them, therefore, must be more or less desirable also. Legal initiatives are important, surely, but only as part of a larger integrated plan.

19.   Many of the ideas enumerated here are derived from Falk, *Toward a Legal Regime for Nuclear Weapons*, 28 MCGILL L. J. 519, 537-38 (1963).

20.   Treaty on the Non-Proliferation of Nuclear Weapons, July 1, 1968, 21 U.S.T. 483, T.I.A.S. No. 6839, 729 U.N.T.S. 161, *reprinted in* BASIC DOCUMENTS at 204.

21.   Treaty Between the United States of America and the Union of Soviet Socialist Republics on the Limitation of Anti-Ballistic Missile Systems, May 26, 1972, 23 U.S.T. 3435, T.I.A.S. No. 7503, *reprinted in* BASIC DOCUMENTS at 213.

22.   Protocol for the Prohibition of the Use in War of Asphyxiating, Poisonous or Other Gases, and of Bacteriological Methods and Warfare, Feb. 8, 1928, 26 U.S.T. 571, T.I.A.S. No. 8061, 94 L.N.T.S. 65, *reprinted in* BASIC DOCUMENTS at 136.

23.   Convention on the Prohibition of the Development, Production and Stockpiling of Bacteriological (Biological) and Toxin

Weapons and Their Destruction, Apr. 10, 1972, 26 U.S.T. 583, T.I.A.S. No. 8062, *reprinted in* BASIC DOCUMENTS at 211.

24.   The U.S. use of the United Nations during the Persian Gulf crisis of 1990-1991 reflected in my view a perversion of right process and was not genuinely unilateral. *See* Weston, *Security Council Resolution 678 and Persian Gulf Decision Making: Precarious Legitimacy*, 85 AM. J. INT'l L. 516 (1991).

25.   See my essay cited in note 25, *supra*.

26.   Some of the ideas enumerated here are derived from the *Report of the Independent Commission on Disarmament and Security Issues: Common Security—a Programme for Disarmament,* also known as the "Palme Commission Report," U.N. Doc. A/CN.10/38 (1983).

27.   The ideas enumerated here are derived in part from Sohn, *Peaceful Settlement of Disputes and International Security*, a "preliminary draft" of an unpublished manuscript to the Independent Commission on World Security Alternatives.

28.   For the first two proposals enumerated here I am indebted in part to Arbess and Epstein, *Disarmament Role for the United Nations?*, 41 Bull. Atomic Scientists 26, 28 (May 1985).

29.   Such an agency—an international satellite monitoring agency (ISMA)—was proposed by a special United Nations commission in 1982 to monitor arms control agreements and perform related other functions. While the plan was ultimately blocked by the superpowers, interest in variations on it have grown ever since.

30.   *Supra* note 21.

31.   The need for an international judicial body to try violations of international criminal law, either as a chamber of the International Court of Justice or as an independent entity, has been recognized for years. *See, e.g.*, the Draft Statute for an International Criminal Court prepared under the auspices of the U.N. Commission on International Criminal Jurisdiction in 1953, 9 U.N. GAOR Supp. (No. 12) Annex p. 23, U.N. Doc. A/2645 (1954).

The Rubin Opinion

1.   Cp. excerpts from the pastoral letter of the American Catholic Bishops, *New York Times*, 6 April 1983, with the views of the French Catholic Bishops, *New York Times*, 12 November

1983.

2.   The legislative process in international law is not to be confused with that of municipal law. There exists no international body with general lawmaking competence comparable to a national legislature. The legislative process in international law includes the negotiation of treaties, the practices of states over time which have become accepted as legally required, certain general principles of law accepted universally by states and, as subsidiary means of determining the rules of law, the decisions of tribunals and the most persuasive writings of publicists. See Sir Gerald Fitzmaurice, "Some Problems Regarding the Formal Sources of International Law," in *Symbolae Verzijl* (the Hague: Nijhoff, 1958), p. 153.

3.   6 I.L.M. 521 (1967). The United States is not a party to the Treaty, but is a party to its two protocols. The first was signed by the United States on 25 May 1977 and ratified on 23 November 1981; the second was signed on 1 April 1968 and ratified on 12 May 1971. See U.S. Arms Control and Disarmament Agency, *Arms Control and Disarmament Agreements* (Washington, D.C.: Government Printing Office, 1982), pp. 76-77.

4.   The Antarctic Treaty, 1 December 1959, 402 U.N.T.S. 71, 12 U.S.T. 794, T.I.A.S. No. 1780.

5.   Treaty on the Non-Proliferation of Nuclear Weapons, 1 July 1968, 729 U.N.T.S. 161, 21 U.S.T. 483, T.I.A.S. No. 6939.

6.   Convention on the Prohibition of Bacteriological and Toxin Weapons, 10 April 1972, 26 U.S.T. 583, T.I.A.S. No. 8062.

7.   A question that might be raised at this point although irrelevant to the subject of nuclear weapons is whether the treaty can properly be interpreted to permit developing and stockpiling the means for delivering so-called "binary" poisonous gases. It is, of course, always possible to construe treaty language so narrowly that it loses substance, and the United States almost uniquely among nations has taken this "naive positivist" position when it comes to interpreting its own treaty obligations. But the treaty partners of the United States frequently disagree, and treaty interpretation is not determined by one party alone. Moreover, the United States is fond of citing the "spirit" of its treaties with regard to the actions of its treaty partners taking technically narrow interpretations of their treaty commitments. This is not the place to try to resolve the questions

of interpretation in the particular case of binary poisonous gases.

8.   In connection with the Latin American nuclear free zone created by the Treaty of Tlotelolco cited at note 3 above, there is an Additional Protocol II dated 1 April 1968, under article 3 of which the parties agreed "not to use or threaten to use nuclear weapons against the Contracting Parties" to the Treaty (i.e. the Latin American states). The Protocol was ratified by the five acknowledged nuclear powers—the Republic of China, France, the U.S.S.R., the United Kingdom, and the United States. But the Presidential Proclamation of 11 June 1971 completing the constitutional process to bring the Treaty into force within the United States said that "as regards the undertaking in article 3 of Protocol II not to use or threaten to use nuclear weapons against the Contracting Parties, the United States Government would have to consider that an armed attack by a Contracting Party, in which it was assisted by a nuclear-weapon-state, would be incompatible with the Contracting Party's corresponding obligations under Article 1 of the Treaty," thus, apparently, freeing the United States to use nuclear weapons against the Contracting Party. U.S. Arms Control and Disarmament Agency, *op. cit*, note 3 above 64, 77-78.

9.   Alwyn Freeman, "Remarks in Memorium to Col. Archibald King," Proceedings of the American Society of International Law 1972 66:280-281.

10.   Ryuichi Shimoda et al. vs. The State, reprinted in English translation in *The Japanese Annual of International Law for 1964* 212-252; Leon Friedman, ed., *The Law of War: A Documentary History* (New York: Random House, 1972) 2:1688-1802; digested in 58 *Am. J. Int'l L.* 1016 (1964).

11.   Multilateral Treaty of Peace, 8 September 1951, 136 U.N.T.S. 45, 3 U.S.T. 3169, T.I.A.S. No. 2490. In article 14(b) the Allied Powers waived all reparations claims against Japan except those provided for in the Treaty as a result of political compromises and trade-offs flowing both ways; in article 19(a) Japan waived its equivalent claims, saying in article 19(b) those claims recognized by individual Allied Powers after 2 September 1945.

12.   E.G. Nagendra Singh, *Nuclear Weapons and International Law* (London: Stevens, 1959) esp. pp. 235-240.

13.   Georg Schwarzenberger, *The Legality of Nuclear Weapons*

(London: Stevens, 1958) *passim*.

14.   The Hague Regulations are reprinted in Schindler & Toman, eds., *The Laws of Armed Conflict* (Alphen aan den Rijn: Sijthoff & Noordhoff, 1981), pp. 57, 76-77. The differences in language between the 1899 and 1907 versions are negligible in the passages quoted; I have used the 1907 version. Convention (IV) respecting the Laws and Customs of War on Land, 18 October 1907, 36 Stat. 2277, T.S. No. 539. Professor John H.E.Fried has suggested that the usual English translation of Article 23(e) is in error. The definitive French forbids using *"des arms des projectiles ou des matieres propres a causer des maux superflus,"* which does not imply intention as "calculated" does. "Apt" might have been the better English translation than the word "calculated" used in official American texts. It could make a substantial difference in some cases.

15.   Schindler & Toman, op cit. note 14 above 78, 789. There are many other international documents relating to cultural property, all reinforcing the principles stated in the 1899-1907 Regulations.

16.   The Lotus Case (France v. Turkey), 1927 P.C.I.J., ser. A, No. 20.

17.   The Genocide Convention, 9 December 1948, 78 U.N.T.S. 277.

18.   The documents relating to this peculiar situation are conveniently reprinted and analyzed in W.T. Mallison, Jr., *Submarines in General and Limited Wars*, (Naval War College, *International Law Studies* 1966, "Blue Book" vol. 58) (Washington, D.C.: U.S. Government Printing Office, 1968) 77-91, 192-195.

19.   Hague Rules of Aerial Warfare, December 1922-February 1923, reprinted in Schindler & Toman, op. cit. note 14 above 147.

20.   Convention on Prohibitions of Restrictions on the Use of Certain Conventional Weapons Which May be Deemed to be Excessively Injurious or to Have Indiscriminate Effects, 10 April 1981, U.N. Doc. A/CONF.95/15 dated 27 October 1980, British Command Papers Cmnd. 8370, reprinted in Roberts & Guellf, *Documents on the Laws of War* (Oxford: Clarendon Press, 1982) 469.

21.   Protocol Additional to the Geneva Conventions of 12 August 1949, and Relating to the Protection of Victims of International Armed Conflicts (Protocol I), 8 June 1977, reprinted in

Schindler & Toman, *op. cit.* note14 551.

22. The official reasons are given in the Message from the President transmitting to the Senate for advice and consent Protocol II Additional to the 1949 Geneva Conventions relating to the Victims of Armed Conflict, 100th Cong., 1st Sess., Treaty Doc. 100-02 (Washington: GPO, 1987), reproduced in 26(2) ILM 561 (1987). George Aldrich, Progressive Development of the Laws of War: A Reply to Criticisms of the 1977 Geneva Protocol I, 26 *Va. J. Int'l L.* (1986), points out that the United States "made a formal understanding when it signed the Protocols to the effect that they 'were not intended to have effect on, and do not regulate or prohibit the use of, nuclear weapons" (pp. 718-9). In the formal Statement by Ambassador Aldrich at the close of the Diplomatic conference on June 9, 1977, he said:

> During the course of the Conference we did not discuss the use of nuclear weapons in warfare. We recognize that nuclear weapons are the subject of separate negotiations and agreements, and further that their use in warfare is governed by the present principles of international law. It is the understanding of the United States that the rules established by this Protocol [Protocol I] were not intended to have any effect on and do not regulate or prohibit the use of nuclear weapons.

Whether "the present principles of international law" regulate or forbid the possession or use of nuclear weapons was not addressed. Aldrich, *Report of the United States Delegation to the Diplomatic Conference on the Reaffirmation and Development of International Humanitarian Law Applicable in Armed Conflicts—Fourth Session, September 8, 1977,* Appendix D, pp. 4-5.

23. Quoting Article 51(5)(b).

24. Declaration made on signature, quoted in Schindler & Toman, op. cit. note 14 636.

25. U.S. Army, *FM 27-10: The Law of Land Warfare* (Washington, D.C.: Government Printing Office, 1956, 1963 ed.) 18. para. 35.

26. Quoted in *ibid.* 6, para. 6.

The Weston Opinion

1.   It merits notice that reputable evidence indicates that the Hiroshima and Nagasaki bombings may have lacked military necessity. *See, e.g.*, the United States Strategic Bombing Survey established by the Secretary Of War, U.S. GOV'T PRINTING OFFICE, JAPAN'S STRUGGLE TO END THE WAR (July 1, 1946) at 13:

> Based on a detailed investigation of all the facts and supported by the testimony of the surviving Japanese leaders involved, it is the Survey's opinion that certainly prior to 31 December 1945, and in all probability prior to 1 November 1945, Japan would have surrendered even if the atomic bombs had not been dropped, even if Russia had not entered the war, and even if no invasion had been planned or contemplated.

2.   See Antarctic Treaty, Dec. 1, 1959, arts. I & V, 402 U.N.T.S. 71; Treaty for the Prohibition of Nuclear Weapons in Latin America ("Treaty of Tlatelolco"), Feb. 14, 1967, 634 U.N.T.S. 281, 6 I.L.M. 521 (1967); Treaty on Principles Governing the Activities of States in the Exploration and Use of Outer Space, Including the Moon and Other Celestial Bodies ("Outer Space Treaty"), Jan. 27, 1967, art. IV, 610 U.N.T.S. 205; Treaty on the Emplacement of Nuclear Weapons of Mass Destruction on the Seabed and the Ocean Floor and in the Subsoil Thereof ("Seabed Arms Control Treaty"), Feb. 11, 1971, 10 I.L.M. 146 (1971).

3.   Aug. 5, 1963, 480 U.N.T.S. 43, 2 I.L.M.889 (1963).

4.   Dec. 8, 1987, 88 DEP'T STATE BULL No. 2131, at 24 (February 1988), reprinted in 27 I.L.M. 90 (1988).

5.   1927 P.C.I.J. (ser. A.) No. 10.

6.   22 TRIAL OF THE MAJOR WAR CRIMINALS BEFORE THE INTERNATIONAL MILITARY TRIBUNAL 464 (1948).

7.   For authoritative support, *see, e.g.*, Article 35(2) of Geneva Protocol I Additional Relating to Victims of International Armed Conflict, Report of the Secretary-General on the Fourth Session of the Diplomatic Conference on Reaffirmation and Development of International Humanitarian Law Applicable to Armed Conflicts, Annex I at 30, U.N. Doc. A'32/144, *reprinted in* 16 I.L.M. 1391 (1977) [hereinafter "1977 Geneva Protocol I"]; Article 6 of the London Agreement ("Nuremberg Charter"), Aug. 8, 1945, 82 U.N.T.S. 279; Article 23 of the 1907 Hague Regulations,

Respecting the Laws and Customs of War on Land, Oct. 18, 1907, J. Scott, THE HAGUE CONVENTIONS AND DECLARATIONS OF 1899 AND 1907 100 (3rd ed. 1918) [hereinafter "1907 Hague Regulations"]. *See also* Fundamental Rules of International Humanitarian Law Applicable in Armed Conflicts, Rule 6, 206 INT'L REV. RED CROSS 248, 249 (1978); Resolution on Basic Principles for the Protection of Civilian Populations in Armed Conflicts, G.A. Res. 2444, 23 U.N. GAOR Supp. (No. 18) at 50, U.N. Doc. A/7218 (1968); Declaration on the Prohibition of the Use of Nuclear and Thermo-nuclear Weapons, G.A. Res. 1653, 16 U.N. GAOR Supp. (No. 17) at 4, U.N. Doc. A/5100 (1961); Hague Draft Rules of Aerial Warfare, arts. 22-26, *reprinted in* 17 Am. J. INT'L L. 245 (Supp. 1923); Declaration of Brussels, Aug. 27, 1874, arts. 12-13, *reprinted in* 1 THE LAW OF WAR: A DOCUMENTARY HISTORY 194-96 (L. Friedman ed. 1972).

8.   For authoritative support, *see, e.g.*, Article 48 of 1977 Geneva Protocol I Additional, *supra* note 7. *See also* Geneva Convention No. IV Relative to the Protection of Civilian Persons in Time of War, Aug. 12, 1949, 75 U.N.T.S. 287 [hereinafter "Geneva IV"]; The London Agreement, *supra* note 7, art. 6; 1907 Hague Regulations, *supra* note 7, arts. 25, 27; Resolution on Respect for Human Rights in Armed Conflicts, *supra* note 7; Fundamental Rules of International Humanitarian Law Applicable in Armed Conflicts, *supra* note 7, Rule 7.

9.   For authoritative support, *see, e.g.*, Articles 20, 51, 53 & 55 of 1977 Geneva Protocol I Additional, *supra* note 7. *See also* 1954 Hague Convention for the Protection of Cultural Property in the Event of Armed Conflict, May 14, 1954, 249 U.N.T.S. 215, art. 4(4); Convention No. 1 for the Amelioration of the Condition of the Wounded, Sick and Shipwrecked Members of the Armed Forces at Sea, Aug. 12, 1949, 75 U.N.T.S. 85, art. 47; Convention No. III Relative to the Protection of Prisoners of War, Aug. 12, 1949, 75 U.N.T.S. 135, art. 13; Convention No. IV Relative to the Protection of Civilian Persons in Time of War, *supra* note 8, art. 33.

10.   For authoritative support, *see, e.g.*, Articles 35(3) and 55(1) of the 1977 Geneva Protocol I Additional, *supra* note 7. *See also* Stockholm Declaration of the United Nations Conference on the Human Environment, Report of the U.N. Conference on the Human Environment, Principles 2 & 26, U.N. Doc. A/Conf./48/

14 at 4, 7 (June 5-16, 1972), *reprinted in* 11 I.L.M. 1416 (1972).

11.   For authoritative support, *see, e.g.*, Articles 1-4 & 10 of the Hague Convention (V) Respecting the Rights and Duties of Neutral Powers and Persons in Case of War on Land, Oct. 18, 1907, J. SCOTT, THE HAGUE CONVENTIONS AND DECLARATIONS OF 1899 AND 1907 133 (3rd ed. 1918). *See also* Articles 1 and 2 of the Hague Convention (XIII) Concerning the Rights and Duties of Neutral Powers in Naval War, Oct. 18, 1907, J. SCOTT, THE HAGUE CONVENTIONS AND DECLARATIONS OF 1899 AND 1907 1209 (3rd ed. 1918).

12.   For authoritative support, *see, e.g.*, Protocol for the Prohibition of the Use in War of Asphyxiating. Poisonous and Other Gases, and of Bacteriological Methods of Warfare, June 17, 1925, 94 L.N.T.S. 65 (hereinafter "1925 Geneva Gas Protocol"). *See also* Resolution on the Question of Chemical and Bacteriological (Biological) Weapons, G.A. Res. 2630A, 24 U.N. GAOR Supp. (No. 30) at 16, U.N. Doc. A/7630 (1969); 1907 Hague Regulations, *supra* note 7, art. 23(a); Hague Declaration (IV,2) Concerning Asphyxiating Gases, July 29, 1899, J. SCOTT, THE HAGUE CONVENTIONS AND DECLARATIONS OF 1899 AND 1907 225 (3rd ed. 1918).

13.   U.N. Doc. A/236, at 1144 (1946).

14.   *See* The London Agreement, *supra* note 7.

15.   *See* Convention No. 1 for the Amelioration of the Condition of the Wounded and Sick in Armed Forces in the Field, *supra* note 9, art. 46; Convention No. II for the Amelioration of the Condition of Wounded, Sick and Shipwrecked Members of the Armed Forces at Sea, *supra* note 9, art. 47; Convention No. III relative to the Treatment of Prisoners of War, *supra* note 9, art. 13; Convention No. IV Relative to the Protection of Civilian Persons in Time of War, *supra* note 8, art. 33.

16.   *See* Declaration on the Prohibition of the Use of Nuclear Weapons and Thermo-nuclear Weapons, *supra* note 7, para. 1(a).

17.   *Id.*, para. 1(b).

18.   *Id.*, para. 1(d).

19.   Declaration on the Non-use of Force in International Relations and Permanent Prohibition of the Use of Nuclear Weapons, G.A. Res. 2936, para. 1, 27 U.N. GAOR Supp. (No. 30) at 5, U.N. Doc. A/8370 (1972).

20. *See* Judgment of Dec. 7, 1963, District Court of Tokyo, *translated into English and reprinted in full* in 8 JAP. ANN. INT'L L. 212 (1964).

21. *See infra* note 30 and accompanying text.

22. Resolution XXVIII on the Protection of Civilian Populations Against the Danger of Indiscriminate Warfare, 20th INTERNATIONAL CONFERENCE OF THE RED CROSS, RESOLUTIONS at 21 (Vienna, Oct. 1965), *reprinted* in THE LAWS OF ARMED CONFLICTS: A COLLECTION OF CONVENTIONS, RESOLUTIONS AND OTHER DOCUMENTS 259 (D. Schindler & J. Toman eds. 1988). The resolution was affirmed by the U.N. General Assembly in Resolution 2444 (XXIII), 23 U.N. GAOR Supp. (No. 18) at 50, U.N. Doc. A/7218 (1968). For pertinent comment on the Red Cross resolution and related concerns, *see* Partsch, *A Legal Analysis of the 1973 Statements of the International Committee of the Red Cross Concerning Atomic Warfare*, in LAWYERS AND THE NUCLEAR DEBATE 370 (M. Cohen & M. Gouin eds. 1988).

23. *See, e.g.*, C. BUILDER & M. GRAUBARD, THE INTERNATIONAL LAW OF ARMED CONFLICT: IMPLICATIONS FOR THE CONCEPT OF ASSURED DESTRUCTION (Rand Publication Series R-28044-FF, 1982); E. CASTREN, THE PRESENT LAW OF WAR AND NEUTRALITY (1954); G. DRAPER, THE RED CROSS CONVENTIONS (1958); G. SCHWARZENBERGER, THE LEGALITY OF NUCLEAR WEAPONS (1958); N. SINGH, NUCLEAR WEAPONS AND INTERNATIONAL LAW (1959); J. SPAIGHT, THE ATOMIC PROBLEM (1948); Arbess, *The International Law of Armed Conflict in Light of Contemporary Deterrence Strategies: Empty Promises or Meaningful Restraint?*, 30 MCGILL L. J. 89 (1984); Brownlie, *Some Legal Aspects of Use of Nuclear Weapons*, 14 INT'L 7 COMP. L. Q. 437 (1965); Castren, *The Illegality of Nuclear Weapons*, 3 U. TOL. L. REV. 89 (1971); David, *A propos de certaines justifications theoriques a l'emploie de l'arme nucleaire*, in ETUDES ES ESSAIS SUR LE DROIT INTERNATIONAL HUMANITAIRE ET SUR LES PRINCIPES DE LA CROIX-ROUGE EN L'HONNEUR DE JEAN PICTET 325 (1984); Falk, Meyrowitz & Sanderson, *Nuclear Weapons and International Law*, 20 IND. J. INT'L L. 541 (1980); Fried, *International Law Prohibiting the First Use of Nuclear Weapons: Existing*

Prohibitions in International Law, 12 BULL. PEACE PROPOS-
ALS 21 (1981) and *International Law Prohibits the First Use of
Nuclear Weapons* , 1 REV. BELGE DROIT INT'L 33 (1981);
Fujita, *First Use of Nuclear Weapons: Nuclear Strategy vs.
International Law*, 3 KANSAI U. REV. L. & POL. 57 (1982);
Grief, *The Legality of Nuclear Weapons* in NUCLEAR WEAP-
ONS AND INTERNATIONAL LAW 22 (I. Pogany ed. 1987);
Kalshoven, *Arms, Armament and International Law*, 191
RECEUIL DES COURS 286 (III-1985); Kennedy, *A Critique of
United States Nuclear Deterrence Theory*, 9 BROOKLYN J.
INT'L L. 35 (1983); E. Meyrowitz, *The Law of War and Nuclear
Weapons*, in NUCLEAR WEAPONS AND THE LAW 19 (A.
Miller & M. Feinreider eds. 1984); H. Meyrowitz, *Le Regime des
Armes Nucleaires Selon le Droit de la Guerre*, in LAWYERS AND
THE NUCLEAR DEBATE 378 (M. Cohen & M. Gouin eds. 1988)
and *Les juristes devant l'arme nucleaire*, 67 REV. GEN. INT'L
PUB. 820 (1963); Shaw, *Nuclear Weapons and International
Law*, in NUCLEAR WEAPONS AND INTERNATIONAL LAW
1 (I. Pogany ed. 1987).

24. *See* 1907 Hague Convention IV, *supra* note 7, preamble;
1949 Geneva Convention I, *supra* note 9, art. 63; 1949 Geneva
Convention II, *supra* note 9, art. 62; 1949 Geneva Convention
III, *supra* note 9, art. 142; 1949 Geneva Convention IV, *supra*
note 8, art. 158; 1977 Protocol I, *supra* note 7, art. 1; and Protocol
II Additional Relating to the Protection of Victims on Non-
International Armed Conflicts, U.N. Doc. A/32/144, Annex II,
art. 1, *reprinted in* 16 I.L.M. 1442 (1977).

25. *Supra* note 8.

26. *See, e.g.*, E. CASTREN, *supra* note 23, at 207; M.
GREENSPAN, *supra* note 23, at 372-73; G.
SCHWARZENBERGER, *supra* note 23, at 37-38; N. SINGH,
supra note 23, at 162-66; Falk, Meyrowitz & Sanderson, *supra*
note 23, at 563; H. Meyrowitz, *supra* note 23, at 842.

27. Fried, *supra* note 23, at 28.

28. *Supra* note 6.

29. *See* National Conference of Catholic Bishops, *The Challenge of Peace: God's Promise and Our Response* (Pastoral Letter
on War, Armaments and Peace), 13 ORIGINS—NC DOCU-
MENTARY SERVICE NO. 1 (May 19, 1983).

30. The ICRC played a major role, as is well known, in the

drafting and negotiation of the four 1949 Geneva Conventions, *supra notes* 4 & 5, and the two 1977 Geneva Protocols Additional to the 1949 Conventions, *supra* notes 7 and 24.

31. *Supra* note 23. *See also* to similar effect the Associated Press and TASS press releases of April 8, 1988 and April 10, 1988, respectively, announcing the formation of the International Association of Lawyers Against Nuclear Arms (IALANA), each available through the Lawyers Committee on Nuclear Policy (New York City).

32. *See, e.g.*, the 1972 Resolution on Non-Use of Force in International Relations and Permanent Prohibition on the Use of Nuclear Weapons, *supra* note 19; 1961 Declaration on the Prohibition of the Use of Nuclear and Thermo-nuclear Weapons, *supra* note 7.   See also Resolution on Non-use of Nuclear Weapons and Prevention of Nuclear War, G.A. Res. 39/92 I (XXXVI), U.N. Doc. A/Res/36/92, at 12-13 (1981); Resolution on Non-use of Nuclear Weapons and Prevention of Nuclear War, G.A. Res. 35/152D (XXXV), 35 U.N. GAOR Supp. (No. 48) at 69, U.N. Doc. A/35/48 (1980); Resolution on Non-use of Nuclear Weapons and Prevention of Nuclear War, G.A. Res. 34/83G (XXXIV), 34 U.N. GAOR Supp. (No. 46) at 56, U.N. Doc. A/34/46 (1979); Resolution on Non-use of Nuclear Weapons and Prevention of Nuclear War, G.A. Res. 33/71B (XXXIII), 33 U.N. GAOR Supp. (No. 45) at 48, U.N. Doc. A/33/45 (1978).

33. *Reprinted in* U.N. Doc. CD/549 (February 6, 1985).

34. *See, e.g.*, the United States Strategic Bombing Survey, *supra* note 1. *See generally also* G. ALPEROVITZ, ATOMIC DIPLOMACY: HIROSHIMA AND POTSDAM (1965); Baldwin, *The Atomic Bomb—The Penalty of Expediency,* in HIROSHIMA: THE DECISION TO USE THE A-BOMB (E. Fogelman ed. 1964).

35. *See, e.g.*, J. ROSE, THE EVOLUTION OF U.S. ARMY NUCLEAR DOCTRINE, 1945-1980 (1980).

36. *See, e.g.*, U.S. DEP'T OF THE AIR FORCE, INTERNA- TIONAL LAW—THE CONDUCT OF ARMED CONFLICT AND AIR OPERATIONS (AFP. 110-31, Nov. 19, 1976) at 5-17 n. 18; 2 U.S. DEP'T OF THE ARMY, INTERNATIONAL LAW 42-44 (DA PAM 27-161-2, Oct. 13, 1962); U.K. MANUAL OF MILI- TARY LAW para. 113 (1958); U.S. DEP'T OF THE ARMY, THE LAW OF LAND WARFARE, FIELD MANUAL No. 27-10, para.

35 (1956) (especially the unpublished annotation discussed in 2 U.S. DEP'T OF THE ARMY, INTERNATIONAL LAW 42-44, s*upra*); U.S. DEP'T OF THE NAVY, LAW OF NAVAL WAR-FARE 613 n. 1, *reprinted in* R. TUCKER, THE LAW OF WAR AND NEUTRALITY, Appendix (1955).

37. *See, e.g.*, Article 22 of the 1907 Hague Regulations, *supra* note 7, which provides that "[t]he right of belligerents to adopt means of injuring the enemy is not unlimited." *See also* 1977 Geneva Protocol I Additional, *supra* note 7, art. 35(1); Resolution on Respect for Human Rights in Armed Conflicts, *supra* note 7.

38. G.A. Res. 217A (III), U.N. Doc. A/810 at 71 (1948). Article 28 reads: "Everyone is entitled to a social and international order in which the rights and freedoms set forth in this Declaration can be fully realized." *Id.* at 76.

39. *Supra* note 7.

40. *See* 1 INTERNATIONAL MILITARY TRIBUNAL, TRIAL OF THE MAJOR WAR CRIMINALS 171 (1947).

41. Dec. 9, 1948, 78 U.N.T.S. 277.

42. June 26, 1945, 1976 Y.B.U.N. 1043.

43. *See* Resolution on the Definition of Aggression, Dec. 14, 1974, U.N.G.A. Res. 3314 (XXIX), 29 U.N. GAOR, Supp. (No. 31) 142, U.N. Doc. A/9631 (1975); Declaration on Principles of International Law Concerning Friendly Relations and Cooperation Among States in Accordance with the Charter of the United Nations, Oct. 24, 1970, U.N.G.A. Res. 2625 (XXV), 25 U.N. GAOR, Supp. (No. 28) 121, U.N. Doc. A.8028 (1971); Declaration on the Inadmissibility of Intervention in the Domestic Affairs of States and the Protection of Their Independence and Sovereignty, Dec. 21, 1965, U.N.G.A. Res. 2131 (XX), 20 U.N. GAOR, Supp. (no. 14) 11, U.N. Doc. A/6014 (1966). These basic instruments were adopted by the General Assembly by consensus.

44. *Supra* note 2.

45. *Supra* note 3.

46. *Supra* note 2.

47. *Supra* note 2.

48. *Supra* note 2.

49. G.A. Res. 34/68 (Dec. 5, 1979), *reprinted in* 18 I.L.M. 1434 (1979).

50. *Supra* note 42.

51. *Supra* note 43.

52. *Supra* note 43.
53. *Supra* note 43.
54. *Supra* note 42.
55. *Supra* note 7.
56. *Cf.* Sadurska, Threats of Force, 82 AM. J. INT'L L. 239 (1988).